WRITERS REPUBLIC

Hiking and Discovering
IN
ENGLAND

BOOK 1 -

EXPLORING
THE NORTH

Linda Loder

This publication contains the opinions and ideas of its author. It is intended to provide helpful and informative material on the subjects addressed in the publication. The author and publisher specifically disclaim all responsibility for any liability, loss, or risk, personal or otherwise, which is incurred as a consequence, directly or indirectly, of the use and application of any of the contents of this book.

WRITERS REPUBLIC L.L.C.
515 Summit Ave. Unit R1
Union City, NJ 07087, USA

Website: *www.writersrepublic.com*
Hotline: *1-877-656-6838*
Email: *info@writersrepublic.com*

Ordering Information:
Quantity sales. Special discounts are available on quantity purchases by corporations, associations, and others. For details, contact the publisher at the address above.

Library of Congress Control Number:	2021912338	
ISBN-13:	978-1-63728-463-6	[Paperback Edition]
	978-1-63728-464-3	[Digital Edition]

Rev. date: 06/14/2021

DEDICATION

To Trevor, my partner and travel buddy who helped make it all happen.

PREFACE

As I sit at the computer pondering our lost holiday due to a worldwide pandemic, I remember all the holidays that have preceded it and feel grateful to have those memories in photos and in mind to enjoy until we can again leave the country to "travel" to places far and near.

Being confined at this time is necessary to contain the spread of the virus but, as people, we are not meant to be confined. We are meant to look out at our world, to explore and discover, not to remain insular and confined in a narrow world of routine and responsibilities. Thankfully, our mind does not need to be confined and we can still look for possibilities in travel once the restrictions are lifted and we are again free to explore.

This time period also allows us to ponder the importance of travel to discover who we are and what is important to us. Without this chance to look out and see other options than the ones that surround us, we remain oblivious to alternative ways of doing things, other perspectives in living and being.

Personally, while I have spent my adult life in Canada absorbing North American values of acquisition, big homes, big cars, big cities and big distances needed to travel everywhere, the notions that I grew up with were surface and did not penetrate into the core of my character. I feel most at home with "small scale, short distances, moderate living and minimalist values. I did not realize this until in 1970 I took my first trip to Britain. I found then, and in many later trips, that I feel most at home away from crowds, out in nature, driving short distances and living in small cottages. While I appreciate my standard of living in Canada, I also cherish the ability to nurture my soul in the alternative spaces that I have found in the countryside of England and Wales. I love the spaces and traces of our history found on the landscape. I love the walking paths scattered generously throughout the land. I love the nearness of nature when we have often shared our hiking with sheep, horses, cattle, rabbits and birds as they live their life and let us pass by. I love to *"Discover"* the secrets of history found on the landscape and the historical heroes and literary giants who have helped shape us and our present.

To make these discoveries one needs to walk and not whizz by on the Motorway. One needs to slowly unravel the secrets of nature that we discover on our walks - the plants, the animals, the secrets of an industrial and geological past which has left its imprint. To me it is a thumb print attitude to exploring. A thumb print placed on a big map covers very little territory but within its confines you can find the treasures of nature and relics of bygone days that inspire curiosity and the need to know more. However, this slow travel is only possible in a society that has had centuries to hone its historical imprint and the foresight to preserve it for future generations in its parks and paths and historical monuments.

Europe offers this perspective and in particular, Britain which has been the country that most inspires us to return again and again. It is this country that I would like to introduce to you in prose and pictures. We anxiously await the time when we can next visit it and in the meantime, I want to share with you a vicarious experience of *"Hiking in England"* and *"The Joy of Discovery"*.

Within this book, *"Hiking and Discovering"* in **England**, I'd like to introduce you to the possibilities of hiking the many beautiful paths both inland and along the coast of this island country. These paths are well marked, well documented, open to the public and are not the private enclaves of developers and the wealthy. They are also easily accessed and do not require the stamina and fitness of a super athlete.

To name a few of the coastal paths: there is the *South West Coastal Path*, located mainly along the coasts of Dorset, Devon and Cornwall, *The North Coast of Norfolk* and *The Eastern coast of Yorkshire*. These paths have everything one could want in hiking including the relaxing presence of the sea, beautiful scenery, wildlife aplenty and access to the comforts of occasional pit stops at cafes in small villages found along their length.

There are also inland paths through the *Yorkshire Dales and the Yorkshire Moors; the hills and mountains of the Lake District; the hills of the Peak District in the Midlands and through the rolling wolds of the Cotswold's and Shropshire Hills.* It is all beautiful and all accessible to those who want to enjoy the great outdoors while keeping fit and free from the crowds and cost associated with many arranged holidays.

Choosing to hike on vacation was a decision which emerged from a few different factors. While we love to hike and be outdoors, we personally needed to *re-balance our life. We had come through a period of upheaval and in order to feel more in control of our life, we wanted to focus on an activity that our minds and our bodies could benefit from on many levels.* This was achieved and we look back on our holidays with considerable pride and pleasure. They represent the pride of achievement, the enjoyment of planning and the joys of hiking in unparalleled beauty in the British countryside. What a journey it was and continues to be as we choose new hiking goals during our holiday time in England.

There was however, a personal journey for us to take before we could get to the point of feeling we could undertake this type of vacation. It was a journey of several years in which we divested ourselves of the North American holiday pattern of "The Road Trip." and invested in the idea of a hiking holiday where we could travel slowly and independently. When we could walk rather than drive, think small area rather than large continent and be independent rather than have the guided experience which is so popular in our society. We had to step out of the herd and go our own way. We are SO terribly grateful that we did.

The North:

Yorkshire Dales, Yorkshire Moors, Lake District
and the Peak District:

TABLE OF CONTENTS:

What follows is a look at our journey to forge our own adventures in hiking in England. A journey which started with a "road trip" and car orientation of BIG travel to a more body friendly and spirit friendly "Boots On" way of thinking. In so doing, we discovered much about our history, our world and ourselves. It was certainly a journey which we wouldn't have missed for the world.

PART 1: THE JOURNEY BEGINS - 1970:

It was a fairly long journey to upgrade my travel IQ and this is how it happened. Way back when, it seems a lifetime away, I went on my first overseas holiday with my Mother. It was to England. We had thirteen days at the end of summer before I returned to teaching, to explore what was my Mother's homeland and my curiosity. We rented a car and proceeded to do "the road trip", in England. It was the first and only time I have done that in Britain.

We shared the driving and proceeded from London as far north as Loch Ness and back again, stopping along the way. We looked up some old uncles of my Mother's in Lincoln, stayed in B&B's, and drove the entire length of the country. Despite this inauspicious start to my exploration of England/ Scotland, I felt at home there. What landscape I saw, I liked; the afternoon teas were delicious; the people friendly and the aspects of history that we came upon in the form of castles were fascinating. We covered a lot of territory in those thirteen days. Mum loved the woolen mills in Scotland and purchased what she could carry home in her luggage. We both bought kilts, of course. I also purchased "haggis" and not realizing it had to be refrigerated, found it uneatable once we were home. I have never tasted or purchased haggis since.

I was young. I did not expect that driving on the left would be a problem. It wasn't. We often fear things more as we grow older. When I returned to it after many years, it was still OK though in my mind I was still slightly nervous.

In our hurried road trip I learned that I wanted to go back and see the things we missed on this whirlwind holiday. I felt at home here. The culture I could relate to, having grown up reading Enid Blyton books whose settings were inevitably in Britain. All my significant relatives were English except my Dad who was born in Canada and some even came complete with accents. Our family culture was largely English and because of this I was curious to learn more about my family homeland.

Therefore, despite having had American T.V., Canadian road trips, camping and a father who was decidedly North American in interest and orientation, I leaned more towards a European outlook and most especially England, the homeland of my family and of my ancestors. I even preferred the climate in England where it is moderate as opposed to the extremes of our climate where it is either too hot, too cold or too buggy, especially in the spring. I don't mind rain. I don't like the cold and I certainly don't like the heat and humidity that we have in the summer. A temperature range of 15 - 25 is great and closely resembles the climate of England which is ideal for hiking and exploring on foot.

It is also of considerable advantage to know the language and although some of the accents, especially in lowland Scotland can be impenetrable, we could communicate, ask questions and learn as we went along. We could mingle and merge and that fact is most important if you want to avoid being an outsider and consequently, "a tourist."

This brings me to an interesting point - that of being *"a tourist or a traveller"*.

In order to step out of the herd, one needs to be more of a traveller even though one may do touristy things from time to time. You have to want to explore, to discover and not to have a set agenda but to let your experience unfold as it will. This is not to say, you should not read up about where you are going and do some research. However, if you have a check list, it prevents you from serendipity, happenchance which is when you go off the beaten track to do or discover things that are entirely new to you.

Travelling vs Tourism: *If it is organized, all inclusive and generally advertised in the travel section of your newspaper, it is likely a tourist experience. Great for getaways, a need for pampering or if you don't want the hassle of planning. It is often shorter, though this is not always the case.*

Travelling *is self -organized, independent and not preplanned by someone else. It is often a lot cheaper as well which was a big plus for us. You are usually not organized into a group.*

THE JOURNEY CONTINUES: 1985

Trevor, a mate and fellow traveller had never heard of the South West Coastal Path when we took a two week holiday to England in 1985. This was our first holiday together and it was a two week get-a-way which included hiking. I had an old AA Book of Country Walks, and found a few that looked promising. I wore running shoes, Trevor wore trousers remade as shorts. We had no boots, poles, hiking gear or proper socks. We were complete novices.

One hotel we stayed at (on the recommendation of my parents who had stayed there a few months before), was located in Bossiney, a village up the coast from Tintagel on the North Cornwall coast. It was also located right on the coastal path. From some literature at the hotel, we decided that we could walk up the coast a few miles to Boscastle and take the bus back as a day's activity so off we went.

Overlooking the castle

> An unplanned and unforgetable experience **which led to SO MANY MORE. Serendipity.**

If you are ever tempted to try the *South West Coastal Path*, this is certainly an excellent place to start. I still remember the foxgloves along the path, the vision of the castle half ruined on the coast, the sounds of the sea birds, the crash of the waves and the quaint village of Boscastle with the decorated cottage with the sloping roof. It was all very new, very exciting and very enticing.

Boscastle in 1985

We scorned the return bus and considering ourselves to be very buff, walked back along the coast to the hotel. The entire walk, which apart from a few elevations, was along the cliff tops, on grassy paths and easily done. The distance was likely less than 5 miles each way and we were able to stop for lunch in **Boscastle**. Our first coastal walk made a lasting impression on us, even though we would not return to do it again for many years.

THE JOURNEY CONTINUES: 1994:

Fast forward a few years to 1994 when we were able to return to England. The intervening years were filled with "life". There were a few interesting diversions in France where we travelled with our kids and our holiday pattern continued to be **"The Road Trip"**. Rent a car and pick up accommodation on route which was a combination of camping, small hotels and B&B's. We ate picnic style with take out and snacks to fill our bellies with occasional meals in restaurants. In those days, before the franc converted to Euros, it was relatively reasonable to live this way on a holiday. Whether this would be affordable today is another question.

Life proved to be somewhat taxing and in 1994, burnout kept me from my teaching job. I was on Long Term Disability for a year to regain my perspective and my health. I was to return to teaching half time the following year, but meanwhile, here was a window of opportunity to take a two week holiday in England in May if my parents would stay with our two girls while we were away.

They agreed and we booked for a quick holiday again in the south of England.

This whirlwind holiday, was a mixed bag but contained one memorable day. We were staying in South Devon in the Salcombe area at a place called **Hope Cove** recommended by Trevor's brother. The hotel was forgettable, but our coastal path walk to **Salcombe** and back was not.

> **Note the pack for water.**
> **We're learning!**

It was a glorious day, the coastal scenery was magnificent and we accomplished the walk without maps but with some water carrying gear which was a step forward. This was our second memorable experience hiking on a coastal path in England. We were intrigued and exhilarated by the day and stored it up in our "Memorable Days" box.

The walk along the coast was invigorating with beautiful views over the water and the countryside. Walking the coast is easy - keep the water on your right (or left). Once we arrived in **Salcombe** and found that there were no buses back to our hamlet of Hope Cove, we headed off cross country and as luck would have it, arrived back at our hotel without a problem. At this point in our hiking, we had yet to purchase maps. We asked questions, followed our instincts and looked for signs to help us.

We were again fortunate in our choice of paths. The section from Hope Cove to Salcombe is rightly acclaimed as one of the most scenic of the entire Coast Path. The walker enjoys dramatic drops to the sea, lofty views and inland fields which we discovered on our return journey. The village of **Salcombe** hugs a hill above a boat filled harbour. We discovered later that this section of the Coast Path is 8 miles or 12.9 km. The entire distance we walked is unknown since we went cross country on our return to Hope Cove. It was before the days of FIT BIT or Apple Watches and we had yet to purchase a Pedometer which was the way of determining distance at the time we walked.

The walk was graded as strenuous taking about 4 hours of walking. However, looking back, I did not remember it as such. Some sections of the South West coast were indeed, memorably "strenuous" but this walk did not present itself as such.

Trev pictured in Salcombe in front of a boat filled harbour. A lunch snack before our return to Hope Cove, completed our day.

Step 1 - To Our Slow Travel:

Pre-booking Accommodation:

Up to now, we were doing a Road Trip which was travelling from place to place and picking up accommodation on route. We would check the tourist agency and start the search late in the afternoon to get a suitable place. This took time from our holiday and it also meant we were spending more time in the car and living out of a suitcase. We soon grew tired of that and preferred to unpack and settle in.

Now we decided to book places for a minimum of 2 nights - preferably 3 and have no more 1-night stopovers. We were becoming "slower travellers" - those who spent more time on foot than in the car and who chose a smaller area to explore. I think this trip was the turning point for us in changing our pattern of holiday behavior.

This was to be the last time that we travelled to England without booking our accommodation before our arrival. We decided that with our holiday limited to two weeks, we were wasting precious time, looking for a place to stay each day and vowed thereafter to book in advance. Our increasing use of the internet made this a very viable option in subsequent years. Along with our Air transportation and car rental, we would be able to book some great accommodation as well. Our holiday would also be paid for in advance so the expense of it was spread out over the year which was kinder on the budget.

We also managed to return to **Tintagel** to get reacquainted with the coastal path around the castle that we had visited in 1985. This time we savoured the view from the castle ruins instead of the coast, while enjoying a Cornish pasty in the shelter of the rocks. **Tintagel** itself is rather touristy, but the castle and the scenes along the cliff are not to be forgotten.

We couldn't linger for more than a night but we were certainly glad to have made the effort to return to this now favourite spot.

What we Discovered!

According to legend, Tintagel is the birthplace of King Arthur who is tied to Cornish resistance to the Anglo-Saxon advance. Arthur was first mentioned by Geoffrey of Monmouth in the 12th Century History of the Kings of Britain. The present ruined castle is medieval but there was an earlier habitation on the site believed to be the seat of Cornish royal power - hence the connection with King Arthur.

PART 2: SIDE JOURNEYS IN THE NORTH OF ENGLAND: 1995-1999

We now knew one thing from our two experiences of hiking in England. We wanted to do more of it and do it properly, with boots and maps and gear. We wanted to become hikers and **Explore England with Boots on Ground** rather than by car.

I was back to teaching again which meant holidays were only in July and August, so we decided that we would explore **Yorkshire in the North,** which was where Trevor had been born and had taught for a few years before coming to Canada. For five years we hiked in the **Yorkshire Dales, the Yorkshire Moors, The Lake District and the Peak District** which was en route to the North. We purchased proper hiking boots, bought rain jackets, good socks, hiking pants and shorts and basically geared up. We purchased Ordnance Survey Maps and books and spent our entire holiday hiking on circular trails discovered in those books, learned to use the maps and honed our navigational skills as well as our hiking skills.

What I Discovered:

The path to good health doesn't lie in pills but in fresh air and exercise and being out in nature. Removing yourself from stressors is not a bad idea either. Do something that makes you feel strong and free to be who you are without the pressures to be what people want you to be.

This knowledge led me to an increased desire for information in natural healing, supplements and exercise which continues today. It also led to an increasing scepticism with regards to reliance on drugs and medical intervention when healthy choices of diet and supplements had better results.

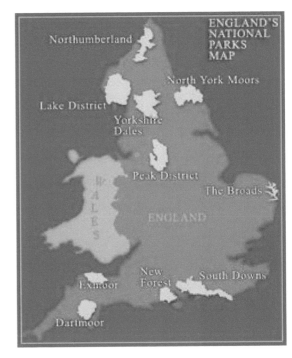

Northern National Parks

THE YORKSHIRE DALES - A TRAINING GROUND FOR HIKING:

Yorkshire to me was "Off the Beaten Track". Mum and I had completely bypassed it on our whirlwind tour in 1970. The only place I had heard of in Yorkshire was the City of York. I didn't know where the Dales were, what they were like, or anything about the area. This was to come. I became educated about the delights of the North and later about its native son, Richard 111 who was a resident here and much loved by the people. He was defeated by Henry Tudor in the Battle of Bosworth in 1485 and by waring factions within his own government.

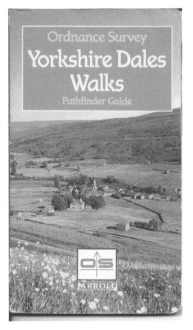

Hiking in Yorkshire for 5 years changed my perspectives about travel and hiking and allowed Trevor and I to contemplate our later quest of hiking the South West Coastal Path. Travel was now "slow" - a small area widely explored.

We geared up. We purchased our hiking boots, clothing and most of all we now had reference material in the form of maps and Pathfinder Guides which guided our experiences on foot.

In Yorkshire, it is all circular walks because you are not following a coastline. Therefore, you need to pay particular attention to your map so as not to get lost. The pathfinder guides were particularly useful since they graded the walks from easy to difficult. As we gained in confidence about how far we could walk, we took longer and longer hikes and enjoyed them all.

Checking my well-thumbed guidebook, I find that we have completed most of the walks as well as many others not mentioned in the guide. Our favourite startup walk was a 6-mile hike into the town of **Grassington** from our accommodation in **Kettlewell.** We would have lunch in the Country Kitchen in Grassington and then hike back. That was 12 delightful miles along the **Dales Way.**

What we Learned:

1. How to hike with the proper gear.

2. How to read a map.

3. What to take with us - water/snacks.

4. How to self-cater in cottages.

5. Confidence in ourselves to do it.

The walks in our guide confined themselves to **North Yorkshire National Park** and the **Dales Way** extended beyond this. No matter. We accomplished what we wanted to do and that was to become hikers, to get fit and to feel comfortable with hiking long distances. We were content and ready to attempt other challenges.

THE JOURNEY TO CHANGE - 1995 +

How did our 5-year experience in Yorkshire, change our travel attitude forever? It did not happen overnight. On our first trip in 1995, we were still staying in B&B's, usually 3+ days at a time. We rented a car in London and headed North stopping in **The Peak District** for 3+ days and continued up to the **Yorkshire Dales, The Lake District, The Yorkshire Moors, York,** and back to **London**. There were no 1-day stopovers on this trip. The next section of this book will look at each of these destinations in turn and show how you can "slowly" travel in the area while enjoying the *hiking and the history* to be found there.

1.   First we Geared Up:

We bought our *hiking boots* -(I got my Merrills in Ambleside in the Lake District.) I remember the store catered to hikers and there were walls of boots to choose from. My blue Merrill boots I had for almost 20 years until the heels fell off within a month of each other. I loved my boots and since they were used for only one month a year, they lasted me very well.

We bought our *rain jackets* during this trip and we still have them. They were the type that rolled up and could be put in your pack. We still take them on every trip.

We purchased *Day Packs* that allowed us to carry with us water bottles, snacks like protein bars and apples and the rain jackets if the weather looked doubtful. It also held our maps and guide book since it was important to refer to these references to avoid getting lost.

Next, we purchased rain pants which turned out NOT to be a good buy. We seldom used them. If it was serious rain, we didn't hike. They also were very hot and uncomfortable so not very useful. I think we finally gave them away.

Last and most important, we purchased **guide books** and **Ordinance Survey maps** which gave us details on the walks we could take and specifics of location needed when we created our own hikes from our accommodation.

2.   Second - we hiked - everywhere:

We usually walked right from our accommodation which was possible in most cases on this trip. There was no need for buses, or the car until it was time to change accommodations. Our car, changed from being what we were in everyday, to what we used only to carry our luggage to our next destination.

We had changed from large scale travel covering hundreds of miles over the course of the holiday, to small scale where we covered only the smallest portion of a very small area in the entire country. Instead of whizzing by in the car glimpsing sights only on the fly, we now had boots on ground for most of the holiday. We could smell the flowers, converse with sheep, hike the trails and explore in real time. Our trip was becoming a **Real Experience** rather than a **Vicarious one** and the funny thing is, we remember it so much more clearly than our cross country races in the car.

The Yorkshire Dales became a familiar stamping ground for us during this time period. We discovered **Bolton Abbey, Middleham Castle,** the home of Richard 111, **Jerveaux Abbey, Malham Tarn, Great Whernside** and all the highlighted spots on the map below. Apart from Middleham, these were all on the **Dales Way - a long distance path of 84 miles** starting in Ilkley and finishing at Bowness -on- Windermere in the Lake District. .

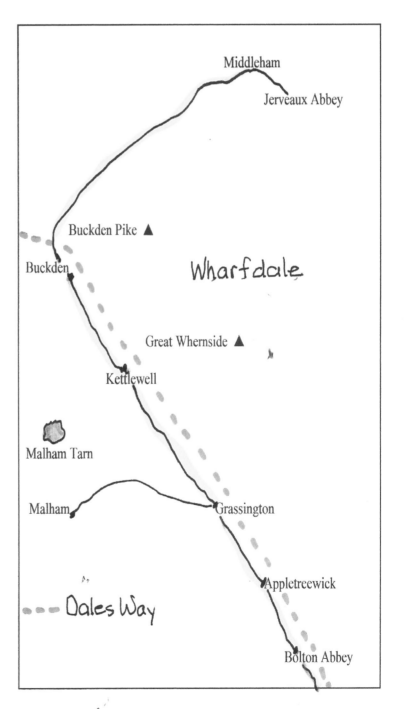

Our hiking adventures were very centered around our accommodation in Kettlewell. It was very easy to climb mountains, visit villages, and do all of the Dales Way in this area without using the car to any great extent.

One memorable walk was from Kettlewell, cross country over to Malham then from there back to Grassington where we expected to catch a bus back to Kettlewell. We were surprised to find that while we wanted to travel to Kettlewell and the schedule said it would, the bus driver had a different view.

"This is the "last bus" and the schedule is wrong". Defeated, we walked the 6 miles back to Kettlewell having clocked over 25 miles in our walk that day. I didn't cook dinner that night. We ate a weary meal in the local pub and came back to put our feet up. Good memory though.

Apart from driving to Middleham. We walked to every spot on the map and back. The walking was easy, except up Great Whernside and Buckden Pike which were mountains located close to Kettlewell. We have been left with many memories of our time in the Dales and countless pictures to remind us of what we have seen. It has made a far greater impression on us, than if we had driven by making the occasional stop which is what we "used to do".

What I Discovered About Memories:

When one gets older and looks back on memories, the ones that stick in your mind are the ones that have most affected you. Boots on ground, close to nature and outdoors and active are the ones that have won out. That is why we keep choosing holidays which allow us this experience and pass on those that are vicarious and distant from personal involvement.

Some memories that remain are those where you have achieved something. When you hike to the top of a mountain and are pictured beside a "cairn" that indicates the top, you are pleased and proud. This "mountain" is **Buckden Pike,** a short distance from Kettlewell. Another mountain to climb in the area is **Great Whernside.** That is the first one we climbed in 1995. This one was gentler and less scrambly if memory serves. We also climbed this one with our daughters in 2003.

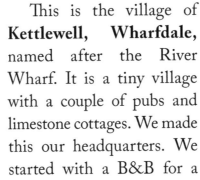

This is the village of **Kettlewell, Wharfdale,** named after the River Wharf. It is a tiny village with a couple of pubs and limestone cottages. We made this our headquarters. We started with a B&B for a couple of years, then found a delightful cottage for 3 years. We also stayed here with our daughters in 2003 and took them hiking.

This is the limestone cottage that we discovered in Kettlewell, and stayed in twice. It was a self contained apartment that had everything we needed for our stay, including parking. The price at the time was £215 for a 6 night stay. Another larger cottage was Polly's Cottage also located in Kettlewell. Not sure if either are still available, but the internet is a good resource.

Malham is an interesting area to explore. There is Malham Tarn, to your right, Gordale Scar an escarpment that one can carefully scale, and lots of Limestone pavements to walk on. The entire area has a lot of offer and is a delight to discover.

Angie, our daughter, with Trevor, scaling the Gordale Scar near Malham in 2003 when we had a family vacation with the girls in England.

Hiking in the Yorkshire Dales is an excellent place to learn how to hike. There is something for everyone in this "Off the Beaten Track" area of Britain. For the Geology buffs, there is the unusual phenomena of "Limestone Pavement" which is found in the Malham region of Wharfdale. **The Yorkshire Dales** is an area of Limestone which is porous and supports only thin soil so it is not good for farming. The water which runs through the area is hard and therefore not good for the woolen industry which requires soft water.

What you can therefore find in the Yorkshire Dales is

* lovely scenery not besmirched with industry and urbanization.

* rolling hills with grazing sheep and limestone walls climbing up the slopes.

* caves hollowed out in the limestone. It is a popular area for "caving".

Angie and Amy walking down from Buckden Pike. The views are expansive, the air clean.
The paths are easily navigated and you can cross the stone walls by means of "stiles," a ladder of stones in the wall.

A Side Trip to Swaledale – Middleham Castle:

Just north of Wharfdale where we had done most of our hiking, we took a day trip and a delightful hike to see the home of a local legend - King Richard 111, whose home had been *Middleham Castle.*

We visited the castle and pondered on the history which lay there. Much later, I was to read up on the history of the late middle ages and learned what I feel was a much more believable tale of King Richard 111, than the one portrayed by Shakespeare who took his information verbatim from Sir Thomas More, who batted for the other side. Richard was well loved in Yorkshire and was considered a good king and just administrator. However, there were too many factions present at court and plots to unseat the King and put Henry Tudor on the throne for him to succeed. His motto was "Loyalty Binds Me" but he was to know little loyalty from the government he inherited from his brother, Edward IV. Richard was just 32 when he was killed in the Battle of Bosworth in 1485.

A pleasant hike from the castle took us to *Jervaulx Abbey* and a perfect opportunity to take more pictures. The abbey was delightfully ruined - "flowers in a crannied wall, arches to peek through to still more arches and a perfect setting for photography. The photo pictured made it onto my easel on our return. While the original was sold, I painted another version of it which we still have in our home. After our visit, we made our way back along the river to *Middleham* again having had a very pleasant and informative day and an easy and attractive walk along the river to the Abbey.

What I Discovered:

This interesting side trip gave me an insight into the life of an important historical figure of the Middle Ages. It aroused my curiosity. I began reading voraciously on the topic and later wrote a course pack on it for my night classes. History that you can see and touch and connect with is another reason why independent travel can touch you when you discover these historical gems tucked away "Off the Beaten Track."

16 x 20 Oil - Jervaulx Abbey

Paintings from the Yorkshire Dales:

11 x 14 – Oil

I have painted several versions of this **"Moorland Sheep"** but the main ideas are there. The photo was taken on our walk back from Grassington to Kettlewell along the "Dales Way". Note the limestone walls, the turf underfoot.

A painting of a Dales Village with the old stone bridge over the River Wharfe. The hills with their stone walls are in the background and a stone cottage by the bridge brings in the human element. **A Dales Cottage by the Bridge:**

16 x 20 – Oil

16 x 20 – Oil

Bridge Over the River Wharfe:

Another painting with a bridge theme since the River Wharfe is ever present in the villages we passed on our hikes. There are also the limestone walls, moss covered in places and the moss-covered graves found by the old church where this photo was taken. I liked the light dancing on the water when I took the photo.

THE YORKSHIRE MOORS + THE CLEVELAND WAY

In 1997 and again in 2003, we included The Yorkshire Moors in our northern adventures and applied the same rules of walking more than driving. We covered much of the Cleveland Way in our rambles especially the distance down the Eastern coast from Saltburn to Ravenscar north of Scarborough. We would like to finish this part of the coast of England but we have confined ourselves to the Southern and western parts of the country in recent years.

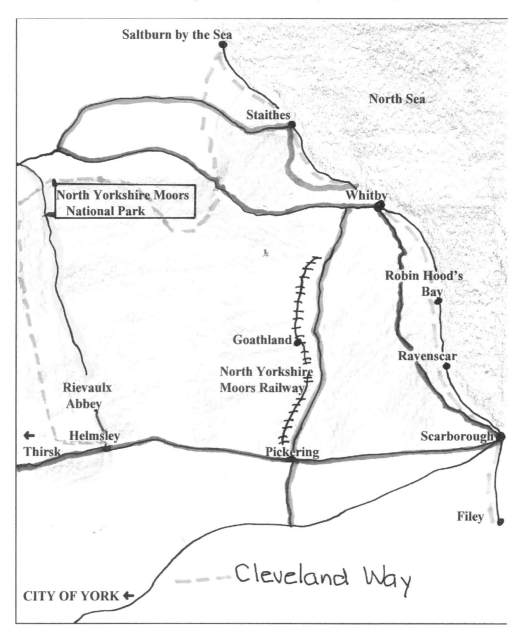

------- The Cleveland Way Coastal - Saltburn by the Sea to Filey

————— A171 - Scarborough North past Whitby

What we Discovered about National Parks:

There is a distinct difference in the National Parks of Great Britain to those of North America. North American Parks are generally areas of scenic beauty with camp sites within the Park boundaries. They were set up to preserve the landscape.

In Great Britain, the parks preserve more than just the landscape, but seek to preserve the cultural heritage within them. There are towns and villages within the park whose development is strictly controlled to preserve the historic appearance of the villages. You cannot tear down and rebuild in a style which does not suit the historical environment. This is delightful as it becomes a cultural experience to visit these towns and villages and not just a photo op. The parks also try to preserve the most scenic parts of the land which is made accessible to the public through public footpaths and maintained trails. The land is open to the public for hiking and enjoyment throughout the year.

Sampling Another Coastline:

The Cleveland Way **is a 108 mile Long Distance Path** which encompasses the sights of moorland, dale and coastal scenery. The area where it is located was designated as a National Park in 1952 in order to preserve the heritage of the beautiful countryside. While we have completed some of the moorland walk the focus here is on the coastal part of Cleveland Way.

Our Experience on the Coastal Trail:

To hike the trail from **Saltburn** to **Ravenscar,** we located our accommodation in Whitby and relied on buses to help us with the return journey. The distance between these two points is 30.6 miles with another 21.4 miles to complete the walk from **Ravenscar** to **Filey.** This is a total of 52 miles.

10 x 20 Oil - Whitby Harbour. This is Whitby Harbour, a photo that later made its way into a painting. The light of the setting sun gave an appealing glow to the buildings.

Whitby - A Good Place to Locate:

This is the jawbone of a whale whose iconic presence is found high on the promenade called "West Cliff" above the town. Here also is where there are many hotels in which to locate. We chose one to stay in for three nights as we walked this part of the coastal path. The sea gulls woke us up early and I remember Trev saying; "I wouldn't want to be married to a sea gull - too noisy in the morning." As they squawked incessantly outside our window.

Here is a statue of Captain James Cook looking out to sea. He is the local hero of the area.

Scenes from the path.

Good walking, well marked and easily done. This day was HOT. We arrived in Robin Hood's Bay and chose to take the bus back to Whitby rather than walk the coastline back.

ROBIN HOOD'S BAY:

The coast of Yorkshire Moors has been designated a National Park as you can see from the previous map. This includes the coastline and the villages and all existing structures. The National Park starts on the coast between Saltburn and Staithes and ends just before reaching Scarborough, its main urban area on the coast. As mentioned previously, National Parks in England preserve the culture and the architecture of the area as well as the landscape. The villages exist as they did in another century so you get a glimpse of what the area historically looked like.

Robin Hood's Bay is one of those "chocolate box" villages that strikes you with a lasting impression. It has narrow winding streets, historical houses and overflowing flower boxes. Following is one of the photos I took of the village when we visited it in July 1996. I have subsequently painted this picture twice - might to so again.

6 x 20 Oil - Robin Hood's Bay

THE YORKSHIRE MOORS:

The Yorkshire Moors have much to interest the hiker and those keen on history and scenery. We are often drawn to areas because of what we have read, seen or heard about them in films, literature or on television. The Yorkshire Moors gained prominence when the T.V. series *"Heartbeat"* was widely watched both in the U.K and in North America. Heartbeat was set in a village called **Ashfordly** which is actually the village of *"Goathland"*, a stop on the **North Yorkshire Moors Railway.** Having watched the programme, we were keen to visit its filming location. Nearby, I discovered a a place called **"Beck Hole"** which inspired a painting shown on the right.

16 x 20 Oil - Beck Hole

Another well-loved T.V. series that highlights this area of England is *"All Creatures Great and Small"*, which depicts the life of a country vet - James Herriot. This series starred Christopher Timothy as the vet James Herriot.

The Vet's Surgery was actually located in *Thirsk* which is a short distance east of the Yorkshire Moors. The photo shows a picture of Alf Wight, the real James Herriot at the surgery during the filming of the series. A new series has started recently on T.V. which again brings to life this lovely section of the world.

On the right is the main street of Thirsk

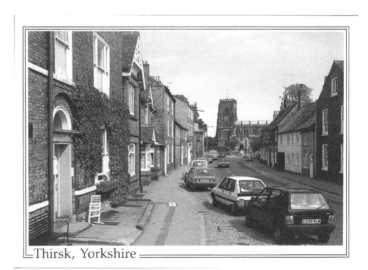

Thirsk, Yorkshire

24

Apart from the delights of the Coastal Path, the **North Yorkshire Moors National Park** is one of the most beautiful parts of England and Wales. It has the largest expanse of heather moorland in the country which can be seen in the photo below.

North York Moors National Park

The Trail is well marked and easily followed with much to see. A Roman Road snakes its way across the moorland, an Abbey at Mount Grace Priory can be explored and a high scenic walk along Sutton Bank are just a few of the sites that can be explored as you hike the Moors.

A Roman road found near Goathland.

Trev pointing to the sign showing the way. It was well marked.

Historically, this is a rich area to explore. **The Cleveland Way** has two abbeys and two castles on route. The trail begins in **Helmsley** where the ruins of **Helmsley Castle** can be explored. It continues a short distance to **Rievaulx Abbey,** an extensive structure well worth a visit. The trail then goes west then north to **Osmotherly** where you can explore the **Mount Grace Priory**.

To give you an idea of the distances for hiking, check the following chart.

Distance Chart for Hiking:		
Helmsley to Rievaulx	2.8 miles	4.5 km
Rievaulx to Sutton Bank	7.4 miles	12 km
Sutton Bank to Osmotherly	11.4 miles	18.4km

We have hiked Helmsley to Rievaulx and Sutton Bank to Osmotherly. The gap in the middle would have to be a there and back as there is no transportation available for us to have returned to base.

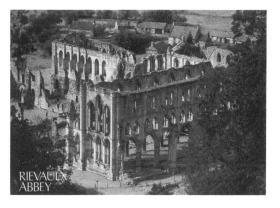

Rievaulx Abbey

Mount Grace Priory

Sutton Bank views from The Cleveland Way path.

Travelling in the North:

The evolution of *our* travel style can be described as having become 70% walking, 20% sightseeing and 10% driving, usually to our next accommodation. We were still staying in B&B's for a duration of 3-4 days, and did not have any 1 night stopovers. It was in 1998 that **we rented our first cottage in Kettlewell - High Fold Lodge**. We had discovered it the previous year and decided to try out the idea of a cottage instead of a B&B.. We rented it again in 1999. When we had the family with us in 2003, we rented a larger cottage in Kettlewell to accommodate 4 people.

We were able to keep our driving distances short because we chose accommodations quite near to each other so we would spend no more that a couple of hours getting there. Since one is not expected to arrive until later in the day at new accommodation to allow for cleaning, we used the en route time to sightsee areas of interest. This allowed us to visit Abbeys, Castles and coffee shops in the area. Indeed, we made the route from accommodation to accommodation in expectation of stopping en route to see something of interest. No driving long distances and only stopping for gas. **The driving was now the "sightseeing part of the trip, " and would remain so for many years.**

The Yorkshire Dales, The Yorkshire Moors and The Lake District are the three northern areas which lend themselves to this small scale travel as you can drive from one area to another with the least amount of distance to cover. They are all National Parks which encourage walking through hiking paths and long distance trails. They all have spectacular scenery and historic sites as well as abundant written material and maps to help with your planning.

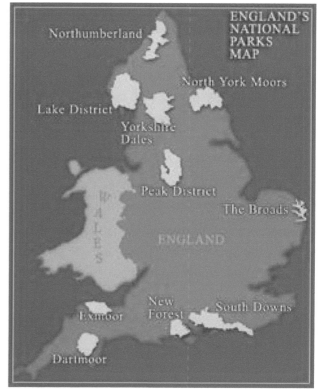

This could constitute your Northern Adventures and because the distances are not large, you could spend more time hiking and less time driving. We never choose to travel both in the South and the North in the same trip since it would require more driving than we care to do. The long trip North to begin your trip and end it, is the longest route that you should be required to contemplate and it can be broken up by exploration in **The Peak District.**

THE LAKE DISTRICT:

We will now progress to the third Northern area to explore and that is **"The Lake District."** In actual fact, this is the best-known area for hiking thanks to the books by Arthur Wainwright who hiked and wrote extensively on the area. We were there in 1995, 1999 and 2003 with the family. To aid our exploration and hiking, we purchased the Pathfinder guide to help us with the trails. We chose to stay centrally in the **Lake Windermere area.** We went again in 2014 to a Time Share we had there, but its northern location away from the walks prevented us from hiking from the door which is what we were used to in previous visits. It was a "drive and see" sort of holiday which we had avoided for many years.

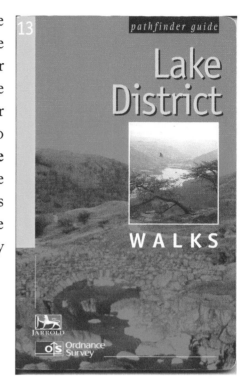

Grasmere, Hawkshead, Windermere Centre Area:

Our favourite area to locate in is from *Grasmere to Bowness-on-Windermere.* We have stayed in **Grasmere, Hawkshead Hill** and **Bowness-on-Windermere**. All locations are centrally located around **Lake Windermere.** There are also two notable worthies who resided here whose histories we could explore.

1. **Beatrice Potter** - lived in **Near Sawry** at Hill Top - a National Trust Property.

2. **William Wordsworth** was a resident of **Grasmere** and later moved to Ambleside. His early cottage and his later home can be visited and you can follow his steps on your hiking adventures.

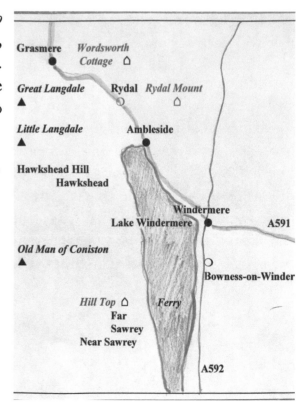

ON THE TRAIL OF WILLIAM WORDSWORTH:

An excellent place to start is in the village of **Grasmere** in the northern part of the previous map. It is the location of Wordsworth's first home which is Dove Cottage and is well worth a visit.

William, and his sister and soul mate Dorothy, were born in 1770 and 1771. William's early years were marked by the death of first his mother then his father five years later. He and Dorothy were shuttled between their grandparents who lived in **Penrith** and other relatives and spent many years apart in separate residences. William and his brother Richard were sent to **Hawkshead Grammar School** in Hawkshead in 1778 when their mother died. They both lodged with Mr. And Mrs. Tyson which is now **Ann Tyson's House** in Hawkshead. They remained at the school even after their father died in 1783. William's literary talent was recognized and he was supported and encouraged. So much so that in 1787 he went to St. Johns, Cambridge to gain a B.A. three years later.

As a young man he toured France and Switzerland and became involved with a young woman, Annette Vellon of Orleans with whom he had a daughter. These were Revolutionary times however, and though he supported and visited Annette when he could, they never married.

He supported another friend who lived near Keswick in the Lake District who was ill with T.B. When the friend died in 1795, he left William a legacy of £900 which enabled he and Dorothy to set up home in Dorset and later in Somerset where they lived near to Samuel Taylor Colleridge.

In 1799, while on holiday in the Lake District, they discovered **Dove Cottage** which was available for rent and decided to return to their roots in the Lake District. Three years later, he was to have a remarkable stroke of luck when he received a legacy of £8,500. The source of this money was from the 2nd Earl of Lonsdale. William's father had lent the 1st Earl a sum of £4-5000 which was interest bearing at 4%. While the 1st Earl had not honoured his debt, the 2nd Earl did and William was the benefactor. This was an enormous amount of money at the time which William and Dorothy benefited from.

As is often the case, William, now in his early thirties and having sewn a few wild oats, decided to settle down and consequently married a former schoolmate, Mary Hutchinson, known from his days in Penrith. He and Mary and his sister Dorothy settled into Dove Cottage together. William and Mary had five children, three surviving. The cottage eventually proved to be too small and after a few moves to other residences, they eventually settled in **Rydal Mount** at Rydal. William meanwhile was employed as a Government Tax agent in **Ambleside** earning £300 per annum. He kept this position until his death at the age of 80 years.

William and his sister Dorothy moved to Dove Cottage in 1799. When Willliam married Mary, she moved into the eight roomed cottage as well. The family remained here until 1808 when they moved to a larger home Allan Bank in Grasmere and later the Grasmere Rectory which is where they lost two of their children, likely due to the dampness of the environment as it was adjacent to the river.

Dove Cottage is open to the public and contains an adjacent Wordsworth Museum which contains manuscripts and paintings acquired from the Wordsworth Trust run by descendants of William and Mary Wordsworth.

Rydal Mount:

The family spent the years from 1813 to 1850 in this large and impressive home with its 4-acre garden. It is run by the poet's descendants and depends on the income from visitors for the upkeep of the home. Moving here coincides with William's new job as a "Distributor of Stamps" which he held for 30 years until 1843.

He then became Poet Laureate until his death at 80 years of age in 1850. He is buried in Grasmere Church.

When we last visited the trail of William Wordsworth, we got a joint ticket for the two properties above. There is a lovely tea room in Rydal Mount and the gardens are great to explore. There is a 5 ½ mile circular walk from Grasmere to Rydal featured in the Pathfinder Series which covers these two sites and the scenery in between.

ON THE TRAIL OF BEATRIX POTTER:

Beatrice Potter was one of the most important benefactors of the Lake District. She was born in London to wealthy parents and was raised by nannies and a governess. She was a solitary child with a talent for drawing and painting and a love of animals which she kept in the school room of their home. These early talents soon morphed into writing and she became an author of some renown, publishing books and earning royalties.

Family holidays had often been in the Lake District so when she became financially independent, she decided to go back there. She purchased **Hill Top** in **Near Sawry** and spent much of the year there. She became an excellent farmer as well as an author and spent her money acquiring cottages and land to preserve it for future generations. She married at age 49 and she and her husband, William Heelis worked together to manage their properties and raise their livestock. Farming eventually became more important than writing, but her contribution to the Lake District is immense. She donated her first property, **Hill Top Farm in Near Sawry,** to the **National Trust**. In **Hawkshead,** property which was once her husband's office, has an exhibition of her illustrations for her little books. The World of Beatrix Potter Attraction is located in **Bowness-on-Windermere.**

In her attempts to save the countryside, she purchased the beautiful **Troutbeck Park Farm** with 2000 acres in 1924. Six years later she acquired **Monk Coniston Estate**, half of which she offered, at cost, to the National Trust. They in turn asked her to manage the estate for them. Cottages she bought on the Monk Coniston Estate in 1930, she offered free to the National Trust. This generosity was fueled by her desire to save the land for the nation so that others could enjoy the landscape as she had for so many years.

Hill Top Farm A National Trust Property

The National Trust is a National Treasure. The generous donations made of property and land to this organization has preserved the U.K.'s heritage for future generations. Without it, developers would have moved in and put profit ahead of preservation as has happened in so many other countries around the world.

PERSONAL MEMORIES IN THE LAKE DISTRICT:

Memories of a circular walk from Bowness- on- Windermere to Hill Top and back.

On the ferry from Bowness at the beginning of the walk with our daughters Angie and Amy.

A stop for photos atop a rock. Lake Windermere is in the background. This walk wasn't in the Pathfinder guide. We used Ordinance Survey maps to guide our way. Easy walking and lovely day.

I used this photo a lot. It was the one on our web site and in the travel guides that I wrote between 2001-2004.

We were lucky to have had excellent weather on all three trips to the Lake District. This enabled long day hikes. Hawkshead Hill circular included Wray Castle where Beatrix Potter stayed on holiday. Grasmere to Ambleside via Langdale Peaks and the day long hike with the girls to Hill Top from Bowness -on-Windermere gave us special memories. Smaller hikes to Tarn Howes and a walk from Coniston around the Old Man of Coniston gave us more good memories of our time in this part of the Lake District.

Paintings from our time in The Lake District:

11 x 14 Oil

This painting called "The Open Gate", comes from a photo taken on our walk to Hill Top in 2003 with the girls. This was a typical scene with the stone walls, the sheep in the fields and the hills in the background. It was a delightful walk.

This painting actually came from a postcard titled "Moonlight Over Ullswater" I liked the mood of the painting of a couple looking out over the moonlit lake.

11 x 14 Oil

12 x 16 - Oil

This painting is called Langdale Pikes and was painted from a photo taken when we walked from Grasmere to Ambleside past the Langdale Pikes on route. The lake in the foreground and the mountains in the distance is again typically Lake District.

16 x 20 – Oil

Castlerigg Stone Circle - near Keswick:

We discovered this prehistoric stone circle on our trip in 2003. It is one of 1,300 stone circles in the British Isles and Brittany. It was constructed during the Late Neolithic and Early Bronze Ages. It was impressive both in its location and size. I remember reading on one of the plaques that it was used as a "wife exchange" area?? If a man was not satisfied with his chosen (or chosen for him partner), he could bring her to this stone circle and hope to exchange her for a more satisfactory model. It never ceases to amaze me of the indignities that women have had to deal with, "forever". Anyway, it was a memorable visit and it resulted in this painting.

Final Notes on The Lake District:

In our three trips to this area, we saw a great deal to interest us and had some amazing walks. The area we stayed is at the heart of the Lake District and is the most touristy because of the many attractions. The number of attractions we saw meant that our ratio of visits to walks changed to favour visits. Instead of 70% walking to 20 % visiting, it was more 50 - 50 here. Accommodation included 1 cottage, 1 two-bedroom timeshare and 1 B&B. The weather can be an issue here but we visited in the summer and enjoyed lovely, warm weather so we were lucky. Well recommended if you want to enjoy the sites as well as hike the trails.

THE CITY OF YORK:

Gateway to the North of England:

Before we leave the north, we would be remiss in not visiting the historical city of York. This city should be on everyone's agenda since it has such a rich historical background.

My first look at York was in **1970** when I explored the famed **medieval walls** with my Mother. On the second visit in **1978**, I was accompanied by my two year old daughter who "helped" me to complete a brass rubbing and explore **The Minster.** On both of these visits, we were touring which left us only a day to see York and just enough time to see one thing, have lunch and continue on to our next stop.

Several years later in **1995**, Trevor and I revisited York after hiking in the Yorkshire Dales. On this occasion we stayed longer, enjoyed one of the city tours and took in the atmosphere in **Medieval Shambles.** We also visited the **Jorvik Centre, the ARC (Archaeological Resource Centre) and Barley Hall** all of which were included on a joint ticket. We took home pleasant memories as well as many photos from this visit.

In the summer of **2003,** we again spent some time in this ancient city. This time we focused on attractions we had missed on previous occasions such as **York Castle Museum and Clifford's Tower, a boat cruise, a ghost walk, The Treasurer's House and the Richard 111 Museum. We took tea in Betty's Tearoom, wandered along the medieval walls and discovered the walking paths along the River Ouse.** Rather than taking a quick look at one attraction, we booked in for three days and had much more time to explore and enjoy our stay.

This is what I would recommend to anyone visiting **York**. There is SO much to see, that a quick visit passing through, would not do it justice.

The list of attractions that I have highlighted above is not complete. There is much more. *I would say that an absolute must would be to walk along the medieval walls and view the city from aloft. I remember being impressed with the Dean's Garden by York Minster and enjoying the Richard 111 museum in Monk Bar on that wall. The Jorvik Centre is also a must see in time travel when you are treated to an experience reminiscent of York in the time of the Vikings. The museums are very "hands on" which was fun and absorbing. York Castle gave you experiences in history including the chance to experience life as a Victorian.*

A visit to York is memorable and deserves more of your time than an afternoon stop over. It also allows you to explore a city of historical importance in Britain as well as either giving you an introduction to the Northern Moors and Dales, or a last look at these areas of England before you head south once again.

Lastly, it gives you a most interesting "walk-a-bout", before taking to the A1/M1 and driving some distance before you are able to begin your exploration of **"The Peak District" our next area of interest and discovery in England".**

The ARC (Archaeological Resource Centre) is fun to visit. It is located in a restored medieval church and is the first hands-on archaeological centre in Britain. Visitors can handle real Roman and Viking antiquities and genuine 1000 year old bones as well as explore a Viking's rubbish pit. The ticket to ARC was joined with one to the Jorvik centre so plan on seeing both attractions on the same day.

At 4.8 km (3 miles), **the city walls** are the longest town walls in England. Walking them allows you the unique experience of observing York from an elevated position. You enter the walls through one of the Bars or gateways into the city.

Bootham bar is the only gate that still stands on the site of a Roman one. Parts of its structure date from the 12th Century while the upper two stories were added in the 14th century.

York Minster is England's largest medieval church which was begun in 1220 and completed 250 years later. It houses the largest collection of medieval stained glass in Britain.

1. The Rose Window is found in the south transept. It is said to commemorate the marriage of Henry V11 to Elizabeth of York, signifying the end of the Wars of the Roses.

Boat Tours up the River Ouse gives you a new perspective on the City of York; one from the water. Along the banks of the river are good paths to walk giving exercise and a chance to explore the city further.

Here is a 16 x 20 painting I did of a scene from inside of the **York Castle Museum**. This museum depicts everyday life in a display of a Jacobean dining room, a moorland cottage and of cobbled Kirkgate Street that you can walk down, peering into shop windows and experiencing life as a Victorian. They also have a nice tearoom here.

Here is a map of the wall and the attractions found within its confines. It is good to group your visits to those that have joint tickets or are in close proximity to each other. There is much to see and all of it interesting.

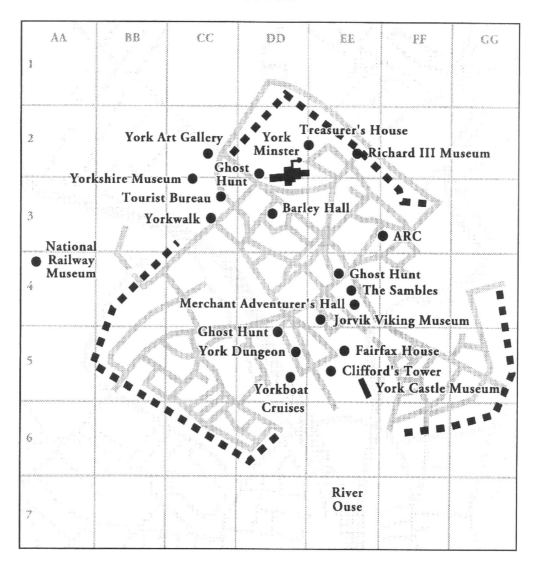

SIGHTSEEING MAP OF YORK'S ATTRACTIONS:

Ghost Hunt – EE4, DD5,DD2

Yorkboat Cruises – DD5

Yorkwalk – CC3

Tourist Bureau – CC3

Jorvik Viking Museum – EE4

Clifford's Tower – EE5

National Railway Museum – AA4

York Art Gallery – CC2

Barley Hall – DD3

Treasurer's House – DD2

York Minster – DD2

Medieval Walls ■ ■ ■ ■

Shambles – EE4

ARC – FF3

York Castle Museum – EE5

Yorkshire Museum – CC3

Richard III Museum – EE2

Fairfax House – EE5

Merchant Adventurer's Hall – EE4

York Dungeon – DD5

THE PEAK DISTRICT:

The Peak District, an area called "**Derbyshire**", is ideally located in the Midlands, which makes it a perfect place to explore after leaving the Northern Parks. No need for a long drive back to the south, but a chance to stop for a few days or a week or longer and enjoy what this National Park has to offer.

It is an area through which the *Pennine Way*, a VERY LONG path through the spine of England, begins. It is also surrounded by large cities such as Manchester, Sheffield and Leeds which makes its presence all the more appreciated by those who can escape to the countryside from their urban enclaves and enjoy nature and the pleasure of hiking in it.

My first view of the area was in 1978. We had rented a van and were heading South from Scotland to return the van to London. We were barrelling down the M5 and were looking for a place we could park the van overnight. Obviously, not on the M roads so we turned off, passed a few towns, one being Macclesfield and headed towards Buxton in the National Park.

The weather suddenly changed. The clouds came in, darkening the sky and the rain began so that it was very difficult to see where we were. We had passed the built-up area and were in open land when I suddenly saw a convenient "pull off" on the side of the road. We took it. We were completely "in a cloud". It was damp, misty and murky everywhere but we were far enough off the road for it to be safe so we decided to stay the night.

The next day dawned bright and sunny and what a surprise! We were high up, with lovely countryside scenes spread out below us. The roads and urbanization that we had left behind had completely disappeared and we were in a beautiful "Shangri-la" a land depicted in the novel "Lost Horizon". I never forgot that experience. My first sight of **"The Peak District."**

For anyone travelling with children, I would highly recommend renting a van. This is a Bedford Van and it served us well. Our little home on wheels was cozy and convenient and it earned its keep that first night in the Peak District. Angie was not quite two at the time and was an excellent traveller both in the van and out of it.

As I discovered later when we continued to visit the Peaks on our way north, The Peak District was the first National Park established in the United Kingdom in 1951. **It is mostly in northern Derbyshire but also includes parts of Cheshire, Greater Manchester, Staffordshire, West Yorkshire and South Yorkshire.**

This is the playground of the populations of the Midlands from the cities of Manchester, Stoke-on-Trent, Derby and Sheffield and it is estimated that 20 million people live within an hour's journey of the Peaks.

Besides wide-open spaces, what attracts people to this area of England? There is a long history of habitation in the area from as far back as the Romans and Anglo-Saxons. There is agriculture and mining which was important from the Middle Ages and later Richard Arkwright built cotton mills at the beginning of the industrial revolution. (Reference - **T.V. drama "North and South"**)

Tourism grew with the advent of the railways and the appeal of the landscape. Visitors flocked to the Spa town of Buxton; Castleton had caves to explore and Bakewell, the only town in the National Park, also attracted its share of visitors.

They also flocked to the country houses and heritage sites that are found in the Park. There are extensive public footpaths, cycle trails, rock climbing and caving and recently, a new 190 mile long-distance trail called "Boundary Walk" which was established **in 2017**. The hiking trails are well documented in the Pathfinder Guide and other references which have helped us plan our hiking excursions on each of our visits.

The Geology of the Peaks:

The Peak District is at the southern end of the Pennines and much of the area is upland and above 1,000'. While there are no sharp peaks, there are rounded hills, plateaus, valleys, limestone gorges and gritstone escarpments. In the Northern part of the Park, there is the Dark Peak which is largely uninhabited moorland and gritstone escarpments. In the Central and Southern White Peak area, there are settlements, farmland and limestone gorges.

The National Park covers 555 square miles and it is the fifth largest national park in England. The National Trust owns about 12% of the land including some of the ecologically or geologically significant areas of the park.

Now that you have a general idea of the nature of the **Peak District National Park**, I am going to focus on the three areas that we have explored, starting with **Buxton**, a town close to where we stopped in the van 42 years ago.

FIRST STOP: BUXTON:

As you can see from the map, Buxton is technically not in the National Park, but it is near enough to it that you are able to walk to the trails. It is also a good place to locate for accommodation if you are interested in doing some hiking. We stayed there for 3 days in 2006 and got in some excellent hiking that we could access from our accommodation or after a short drive.

BUXTON AND ITS HISTORICAL GHOSTS:

Buxton has a long history. It was first settled by **the Romans** as a spa town in AD78. Then it was known as *"Aquae Arnemetiae"* or the spa of the goddess of the Grove.

Fast forward to the Renaissance time period. **Bess of Hardwick** and her husband the Earl of Shrewsbury took the waters in 1569.

Another famous visitor was **Mary, Queen of Scots** who was brought to Buxton by Bess of Hardwick and the Earl in 1573. Mary was under "house arrest" at the time, a rather pleasant one considering her status, while Queen Elizabeth was trying to figure out what to do with her.

Robert Dudley, the Earl of Leicester was on his way to Buxton on the advice of Queen Elizabeth 1 in 1588. He had been involved in the war against the invasion of the Spanish Armada during the summer months and Elizabeth became concerned about his deteriorating health. When he succumbed to his illness at his lodge near Woodstock in Oxfordshire on Sept. 4, 1588, he was en route to Buxton hoping for a cure.

The town grew in importance in the late 18th Century when it was developed by the 5th Duke of Devonshire modelling it on the spa city of Bath. Buxton has its own "Crescent" after the style of Bath's Royal Crescent, and The Natural Baths and Pump Room. Pavilion Gardens were opened in 1871 and an opera house in 1903. It is a pleasant and attractive town to settle in for a few days or a week while enjoying the sights and the hiking nearby.

 Here in Buxton, you are not far from the location of a famous event which took place in 1932 called "The Kinder Trespass." This was an important event in the campaign for open access to moorland in Britain and eventually led to the formation of Britain's national parks. Before the trespass, open moorland was closed to all. Moorland estates were private properties owned by the gentry who used them for 12 days a year while for the remainder of the year they were guarded by their gamekeepers. After the trespass, *The Peak District National Park became the U.K's first national park on April 17, 1951. This was followed by the first long distance footpath in the U.K., the "Pennine Way" which opened in 1965 and led to SO MANY MORE.*

<u>This is an important step in opening up the country for hiking – YEA!</u>

In honour of the opening of the countryside to hikers and ramblers, Buxton itself has a Country Park located on its fringes which can be accessed on foot from Buxton. This is called **"Buxton Country Park"**.

We were staying in a delightful B&B just off a main road and easy to find. Checking the internet, it appears at the time of writing that this accommodation at **9 Green Lane** is still in business and the prices are on a par with others nearby. My notes describe our B&B as "Excellent". It is a Victorian home with its own car park and a spacious interior. We had a table and chairs nestled in a bay window and a full bathroom in ours.

They have 7 rooms which you can book directly on line. The rooms are pictured so you can see which would suit you best. So much more convenient than it used to be!

From here, we could walk directly to the Buxton Country Park and our day's excursion. There was also an Italian Restaurant called "Michael Angelos:" about a 5-minute walk away which we used for our dinners.

Accommodation:

Everyone has their own budget for accommodation. As choices come and go it is best to use the Internet to book a satisfactory place to stay. There are often reviews of the accommodation to help you decide. In recent years on our travels, we have opted for cottages but there are often times when it is necessary to choose B&B's or hotels. When this occurs, usually at the beginning or end of our holiday, we have been choosing the chain *"Premier Inn"*. We have found their prices to be excellent and while they do not provide breakfast, there are always en site restaurants where we can get our continental or cooked selections. The beds are excellent, there is free WIFI, and the rooms are usually a good size. They are, however, uniformly the same. If you want more of a character bedroom, B&B's in converted homes such as the one above, will give you that. They have a single's rate but they usually advertise the price per room rather than per person. If you don't have to buy breakfast then you are likely paying a similar price to Premier Inn. One thing we noticed is that if you stay longer in some hotels, you get a better rate. In both cases however, you will have to eat supper out, so having restaurants or pubs close by is an advantage.

1. BUXTON COUNTRY PARK WALK:

This walk is located on the southern fringes of Buxton and we accessed the park without using our car. If you choose to use the car, parking is at Grin Low car park.

The history of this park goes back to one of the Dukes of Devonshire who organized the planting of trees to hide the waste tips caused by centuries of quarrying and lime-burning. **Grin Quarry** was reclaimed and landscaped as a caravan site as recently as 1982.

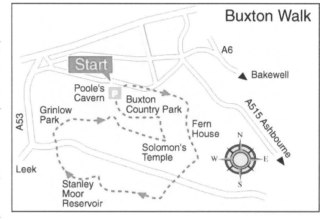

Other features in the park is a tower called **"Solomon's Temple"** built in 1896 by Solomon Mycock to provide work for the unemployed. It stands on a hill 1,440' high and from it you have wonderful views over Buxton.

Heading downhill from this feature in the direction of the town you come to **Grin Woods,** an area of the 100 acres of woodland planted by the Duke in 1820. Continue ahead through the woods and look for the signs to **Poole's Cavern.** This is an impressive natural cave named after an alleged medieval outlaw and historically has yielded up Roman artifacts which indicates its long history.

This is a relatively short walk which takes you in a circle back to Buxton but there is a lot to see. On our walk we came upon a farmer in the process of sheep dipping which was interesting to see. The views were wonderful and although we skipped the cave on our excursion, we enjoyed our afternoon walk immensely.

Here we were heading up towards Solomon's Temple when we saw the sheep.

Here is Solomon's Temple and next to it the view of Buxton down below.

2. Three Shires Walk:

Our second walk from Buxton is mostly over wild moorland and starts from a well-known pub called **"The Cat and Fiddle Inn"** which is known to be the second highest Inn in the UK. This is a fine weather walk since you want to be able to appreciate the expansive views in all directions and the feeling of spaciousness and freedom that you get from experiencing it. The walk and the landscape is reminiscent of my first view of the Peak District in 1978 and indeed this walk is on the route from Macclesfield to Buxton so it is likely what we saw when the clouds lifted and the sun came out.

The title comes from the fact that three counties meet at a half-way point at Three Shires Head, a spot where not only the streams and paths meet at a packhorse bridge, but the counties of Cheshire, Staffordshire and Derbyshire also converge. We had walked mostly alone for most of the day when we suddenly came upon several people grouped on a bridge and milling about. We wondered why? It was later, when we consulted our guide book that we learned about the significance of the location.

We parked at the Inn which is 1,690' high. It was built to serve the new turnpike road completed in 1823, which later became the present A537 - Macclesfield to Buxton route and the one we found ourselves on in 1978. This is a popular area for hikers, bikers and motorists who can all enjoy the expansive scenery from their own choice of transportation - wheels, bikes, foot. The documented hike is #17 in the Pathfinder Guide and is 7 ½ miles or a 4-hour hike.

THREE SHIRES WALK - STARTING POINT:

Here is the starting point of the walk - the second highest pub in England. When we returned a few hours later, there were many hikers and bikers in the parking lot.

Here is an outline map of the walk. I think we did a variation on it but we saw all the sights and of course the moorland scenery which was spectacular. Towards the end of the day, the clouds were coming in as you can see from the pictures above but most of the day was clear and dry.

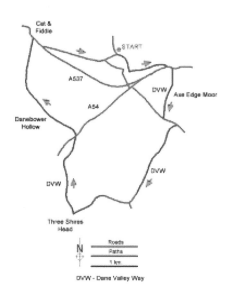

Here we are at the Three Shires meeting place by the Pack Horse Bridge. We asked a fellow hiker to take our picture.

Scenery Shots and Sights Along the Trail:

The scenery was wonderful. Just so expansive as if it could go on forever. Here is Trevor tripping along. Not bad for a 75-year-old.

While hikers were few on the ground, sheep were our constant companions.

Hikers on the trail, some of the few that we saw that day. The paths are clear and easily walked, often on tarmac. The prime thing you will remember are the views and the openness of the landscape. It makes you feel free as you hike in the natural world and are one with nature and the creatures in it - the sheep.

CASTLETON:

Castleton makes an excellent stop for a few days or a week and has several hiking attractions to lure you. We have stayed there at least 3 times on our treks to the North and have enjoyed a variety of experiences on our visits.

Castleton is located at the border of the Southern White Peaks or Limestone Dales and the Northern millstone grit or Black Peak area. I mentioned earlier that the Northern Peaks are comprised of wild, open moorland with little habitation. It is also the start of the *Pennine Way* and the site of *"The Great Trespass"* which was responsible for opening up the land with National Parks and hiking trails. Without this momentous change, Britain would have been subject to the disadvantage of "private lands" which in most other countries prevents citizens from enjoying the freedom to roam. It has made Britain uniquely available to explore on foot and to discover the hidden historic treasures of the landscape. Its citizens and visitors can enjoy the freedom of the outdoors often denied in other countries. It is the reason why we have travelled there so often and continue to enjoy our hiking experiences throughout Britain.

Looking back and relying on memory rather than references is important. What has remained in my memory are the highlights of our visits and therefore worthy of mention. The insignificant has disappeared from our mental map so I will not bother with it.

Castleton

Our accommodation in Castleton was always B&B's as we stayed for 2-3 days on each occasion. This was particularly useful on one occasion when I broke a tooth and our landlady sent me to her dentist to have it fixed. The personal touch is always a pleasure. I would not have had that were we living in a hotel.

Castleton is similar to **Kettlewell** in the Yorkshire Dales. It is a small limestone village with a river running through it and hiking at your doorstep. Most of our walks did not require a car. The walks were memorable, scenic and easily accessed from our accommodation.

THE HIGHLIGHTS OF CASTLETON AREA:

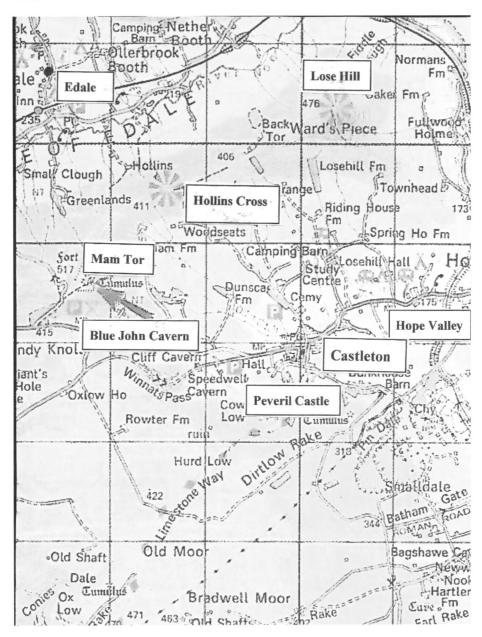

Here is an area map of Castleton showing the highlights from our visits there. To get to **Castleton,** the easiest route is from the East via the M1 to the Sheffield area then west towards Hathersage and the Hope Valley. Getting there from Buxton, the route is more indirect leaving you with no option but taking a circular route many miles out of your way. This is the border area of high moors and mountain passes. There are fewer towns and villages and large tracks of moorland where no transportation exists at all. At **Edale** above, the first long distance trail **"The Pennine Way"** which was opened in 1965, starts across the moors.

Park your car, settle in and enjoy your "on foot" experience in Castleton. The town may be named after the local castle - **Peveril Castle**. This structure dominates the local landscape. The castle, which is in a ruined state, was commissioned by William Peveril in 1086 after he was rewarded for his contributions to the success of William the Conquerer's 1066 invasion of England. This was how supporters were rewarded in a successful campaign - through lands often taken from the locals.

Trev looking out over the ramparts.

The castle is perched high on a crag and is surrounded by fantastic scenery. It looks down on the little market town of Castleton and commands extensive views in all directions which made it an ideal location in uncertain times. The North Side is guarded by a high stone wall which is still complete. The path up to the castle is steep, but the views, once there, make it an exhilarating experience.

Peveril Castle is an **English Heritage** property. I have mentioned National Trust before. There is a second organization whose primary concern is the preservation of Historical buildings. One finds more castles and abbeys with this organization while National Trust has a larger share of property and stately homes.

We have memberships with both organizations so that we are covered and do not have to pay the entrance fees. I should say more about membership.

English Heritage and National Trust manage most of the historical homes and properties you are likely to visit. There are some private properties as well but you are well covered if you have the above memberships. One year, wanting to know whether it was worthwhile for us to get a membership, I added up the costs of our visits and compared them to the cost of a joint membership. There was no contest! We had used up the cost of the membership after only a few properties so we purchased a couple membership for a year for just over £100, which allowed us free access to the sites for the rest of our holiday. We have renewed our memberships every year since that time.

While discovering an ancient castle might be the main item on your agenda, you may also want to view the castle in passing and return to explore it later. There is an information display before ascending to the castle which will give you opening times and cost before you huff and puff up the hill. A nice stroll down Cave Dale allows you a different viewpoint of the castle perched high above you. You can follow the signs for Peak Cavern which takes you to a spectacular cliff side and the entrance to one of the many caves in the area.

BLUE JOHN CAVERN:

The cave we visited was the famous Blue John which mined a mineral called "fluorite". The mineral is scarce and now only a few hundred kilograms are mined each year to create jewellery. I remember purchasing a dark blue pendant - a rather practical souvenir. Blue John is a show cave. The actual mining takes place at another cavern in the area.

The 45-minute descent is accompanied by an informative talk and takes you to the deepest cavern in England. The descent will take you 244 steps down into the depths of the cave and of course back up again. There is free parking at the Cavern if you have taken your car. 100 Metres up the road you will find another attraction not to be missed - The trail to **"Mam Tor" or "The Shivering Mountain"**. The path is well defined and you will end up on the paved top which gives you wonderful views over Edale and the High Peaks beyond. I would however, give a full day to this wonderful hike which I will describe in pictures on the following page.

Reaching Mam Tor from the caves is a short cut, the full and most wonderful hike is on the next page.

CASTLETON AND MAM TOR: #11 IN THE PATHFINDER GUIDE:

This hike starts in Castleton, heads towards Peveril Castle and the Cave Dale route which is a long, steady ascent. After levelling off, it climbs again up to the 1,695' summit of **Mam Tor**. Thereafter, you are treated to the most scenic ridge walk in the Peak District. On one side you have Hope Valley and on the other, the Vale of Edale. The expansive scenes are wonderful. You can continue along this ridge to another peak which is **Hollins Cross** and if you wish, a further peak which is **Lose Hill**. The descent into Castleton mentioned in the designated walk, is at Hollins Cross. Without the extra hike to Lose Hill, the hikes details are as follows:

> **Castleton and Mam Tor Ridge Walk:**
>
> **Start: Castleton**
>
> **Distance: 6 miles (9.5 km)**
>
> **Time to Complete: 3 hours**
>
> **Refreshments: Pubs and cafes in Castleton.**

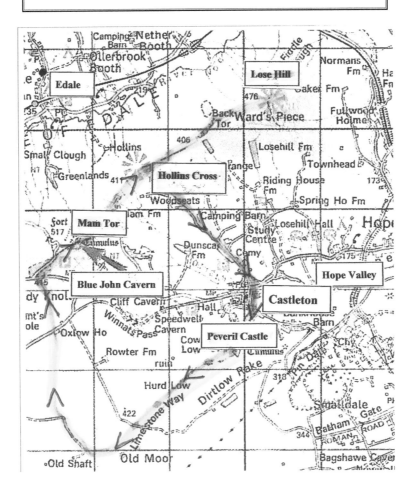

SCENES FROM THE WALK:

This is the path leading from the summit of **Mam Tor**. Wide and paved and easy. The hard part is the climb up to the top before you are rewarded with wonderful views all along this ridge path.

The summits of the three peaks are marked with cairns or piles of rocks to indicate the location of the summit.

The Three Peaks along this route are:

1. Mam Tor
2. Hollins cross
3. Lose Hill

We discovered that Mam Tor goes a long way back - to the Iron Age. It is an ancient hillfort.

This is the view that greets you as you walk along this ridge path. To the left are the open moors and High Peaks of the Northern Peak District wherein lies "The Pennine Way" which starts in Edale. To the right is Hope Valley and Castleton when you decide to descend again after your afternoon of spectacular views.

I remember we walked the full distance up to Lose Hill before we descended into Castleton. This added a few miles to the total but it was certainly worth the effort.

Side Trips from Castleton:

Kinder Scout:

While in the area it is worthwhile to discover what else there is of interest. We've explored a castle, a cave and had a wonderful walk. For the truly ambitious, an exploration of the **Pennine Way** is a suggestion. We hiked over to **Edale** and started on a walk to **Kinder Scout**, an upland point about 2 miles along the path. It started well but was shortened because of weather. We decided to err on the side of caution and returned to Edale and the walk back to Castleton.

A note in our Pathfinder Guide talked about weather and Moorland hiking.

"Featureless moorland presents few route-finding difficulties in good weather, but in bad weather and when visibility is poor, you should not attempt it unless an experienced walker and able to use a compass."

This is the beginning of the "Pennine Way" in Edale. The first part of the trail was good with easy walking.

First the rocks happened and the hiking became very scrabbly.

Then the wind and the rain arrived. We bolted back to Edale and a rainy walk to Castleton.

HATHERSAGE IN SEARCH OF TWO HISTORICAL GHOSTS:

Before continuing south to Bakewell, our third option for a short-term stay, an "en route" stop at **Hathersage,** a few miles east of Castleton would be an excellent choice. Two historical ghosts are associated with this town so let's discover who they are.

In Search of Charlotte Bronte's "Jane Eyre"

While the Bronte sisters are associated with the village of Haworth which is where the Bronte Parsonage Museum is located in their former home, their writings encompass many local areas, one of which is **Hathersage.** In her novel "Jane Eyre", Charlotte Bronte based the fictional village of Morton on Hathersage where she had stayed in 1845. The following postcard I purchased during our visit there, gives you the various associations in Hathersage which come from the novel.

Discovering locations used in literature, T.V. and movies is most interesting. One often goes in search of these locations as part of the experience of travel. This was a discovery we made quite by accident when we visited Hathersage in 1998.

THE LITTLE JOHN CONNECTION:

Hathersage is likely better known as the site of Little John's grave than for anything else. Little John of course was the name of Robin Hood's lieutenant. The churchyard has a large grave beneath the yews in the south-west corner which is labelled that of Little John. To support this claim there are several stories and facts which the public have been made aware of.

1. The Cottage:

There was a cottage which stood at the eastern side of the church until well into the 19th century which was reputed to be the cottage in which Little John died. In 1847 its occupant was a woman of 70 who had the story from her father who had died 20 years earlier at the age of 92. He had the story handed down to him from previous generations.

2. The Thigh Bone:

She also remembered the grave being opened by Captain James Shuttleworth, and a thigh bone which was 32 inches long was discovered. This would indicate a man of seven feet in height. The original grave according to some authorities could have been a 600 year old stone in the porch of the ancient church.

3. The Bow and Cap:

It is also a fact that there was at one time in the church, a long bow and a cap said to have been Little John's. The bow was taken away for safe-keeping by a former squire.

The Churchyard where Little John's purported grave is located. Much circumstantial evidence plus local tradition gives credence to the legend but it will always likely to be open to dispute.

Exploring the Bakewell Area:

Looking back at our visits to the Peak District our experiences in the Bakewell area have been more numerous than in the other two locations. We have been here on at least four occasions during the 90's and later in 2006. The reasons for this are many, but one is Bakewell's easy accessibility. Coming north on the M1, it is a direct route via Chesterfield to get to Bakewell and the villages surrounding it.

A second reason is there are a great many interesting and historical attractions in this area which we wanted to discover.

A third reason, of course, is the hiking.

The accessibility to Bakewell was what brought us here in the first place. The other two reasons kept us coming back. This then is the third place we would recommend locating in if visiting the Peak District. We used to rely on recommended B&B's and without exception, they were excellent and very well placed for walks from the door. Always check the internet for updates however.

Two of the accommodations that we have stayed in are still listed on the Internet - **1. Bole Hill Farm Cottages 2. The Hollow - Little Longstone**. They both come highly recommended by Trip Advisor. Both are comfortable, have character, and are close to the attractions and hiking available in the area.

If you are thinking of staying in a cottage, we have used the following companies on many occasions.

1. Blue Chip Cottages - These cottages are excellent and of high quality with all the extras you would expect.

2. Sykes Cottages - Another company we have used and were very satisfied with the quality of the properties.

3. Trip Advisor - This was the last company we used - the year of Covid 19 in 2020 when our trip was cancelled. We got a full refund for the cottage rental, including the deposit.

Bole Hill Cottages: 5* 2 miles from Bakewell 8 cottages in courtyard setting

1. The Hollow: 5* B&B located close to the Monsal Trail.

We liked these two locations because of their easy accessibility to hiking from the door of the accommodation. **Bole Hill Cottages** gave us easy access to **Lathkill Dale** taking us up to **Monyash.** An interesting day hike right from the door.

The Hollow, was located on the **Monsal Trail,** a disused rail line converted into a footpath that took us into Bakewell in one direction or to **Monsal Head** and beyond in the other.

For these hikes and many others in this area, we used the **"Ordnance Survey Maps".** These maps give great detail - even showing "Bole Hill Farm" on it. This allowed us to follow our own circular path from our accommodation which I highlighted on our map. These maps are excellent for cross country hikes. All the walking paths are found on the map so you are able to create your own trail from your accommodation. They are in a big scale - 4cm to 1km or 2 ½ "to 1 mile so you can also estimate the distance of your walk.

The walk on the next page leaves right from Bole Hill farm indicated by a Red Dot on the map on the next page. It crosses fields following Footpath signs, and then a clearly marked trail along a river in

Lathkill Dale. The village of **Monyash** gave a location for us to stop for lunch in a recommended Teapot Trail café, and then a circular walk back to our B&B. Our return path was along the **"Limestone Way",** again a well-marked path. Our map was essential however, pointing the way to achieve our circular walk distance of your walk.

While you need a map, you also need to be observant in looking for Footpath signs. We

walked up the road a short distance from our accommodation before we were able to see the sign on the right. We followed it looking for others and we gained our objective a few fields on. Without access to a good map, you are in danger of getting lost. We have learned this lesson from our own experiences in hiking. **Always take water, a snack and a good map.**

Lathkill Dale Scenes. The path is obvious and well-marked but you need the Ordnance Survey Map to ensure that you keep on it.

Another landscape detail given by your map is the river, which you follow on your way towards **Monyash**. Once there, you are rewarded by a snack at a café recommended by "The Teapot Trail" booklet before starting on the walk back.

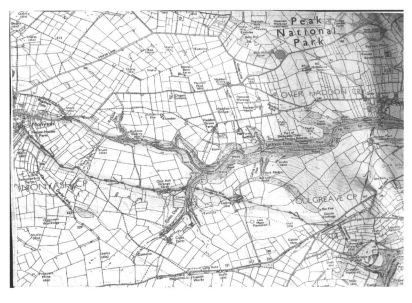

Exploring the Monsal Trail:

"The Hollow" in Little Longstone is located on the Monsal trail which is very convenient for hikers who want to explore this interesting trail.

The Monsal Trail used to be part of the Midland Railway in the 1860's, which extended their services to Manchester. This section of the line passed close by **Haddon Hall**, home of the Duke of Rutland. He insisted that the railway should pass through a tunnel behind his property rather than passing in front of it and spoiling the view. This led to the construction of Haddon Tunnel and a rail line located high above Bakewell and the station uphill from the town centre.

The station was closed in 1967 after 100 years in operation and in 1968, the last train ran on the Midland Line. Twelve years later, the line was taken over by the **Peak District National Park** which turned it into a walking and cycling route called "**The Monsal Trail**".

The Monsal Trail is 24 miles long and generally follows the route of the River Wye towards Buxton. There is a lot to see on the trail and there are many references both on line and in booklets to help plan walks along it and in the surrounding area. We enjoyed our hikes in the area and would locate again in the same spot to take advantage of the proximity of the trail and to avoid the need to use your car.

Here is the **Monsal Trail** which roughly follows the route of the A6 highway. Little Longstone is ideally situated to take advantage of this walking trail.

SITES ALONG THE TRAIL:

1. Monsal Head Viaduct:

A short walk from Little Longstone, is this impressive viaduct. There is a pub and a café at Monsal Head to enjoy after seeing this wonderful view. There is also parking.

Monsal Head Viaduct:

2. Cressbrook Mill:

This mill stands on the site of the original cotton mill established by Richard Arkwright. (North and South T.V. series BBC) Big Mill replaced it and was worked until 1965. It has now been converted into luxury apartments.

Cressbrook Mill:

3. Miller's Dale:

An attractive and easy walk on the **Monsal Trail.** For our walk we parked at Monsal Head and walked up through Miller's Dale and returned to our car by the same route. The trail followed attractive scenery and was easy to follow. Not sure of the mileage but it was a pleasant afternoon walk.

Ashford in the Water, Bakewell and Haddon Hall:

1. Ashford in the Water:

Ashford is one of the most picturesque villages in Derbyshire with limestone cottages lining the streets and a famous site that has made its way into many paintings and calendars, **"The Sheepwash Bridge"**.

It is an old Packhorse bridge which got its name from the fact that sheep were washed in the River Wye here prior to shearing. The farmers would shepherd the ewes across the bridge while the lambs were penned on the other side. Following their motherly instinct, the ewes would then swim back to their bleating lambs on the other side and thereby get a good wash in the process.

You can walk to Ashford from the Monsal trail either from Little Longstone or from Bakewell along the River Wye path. The village is just a couple of miles from Bakewell and has a pub and cafes for a nice break in the walk. The map below shows the locations of the accommodations, the Monsal trail, Bakewell and the connecting roads of the area.

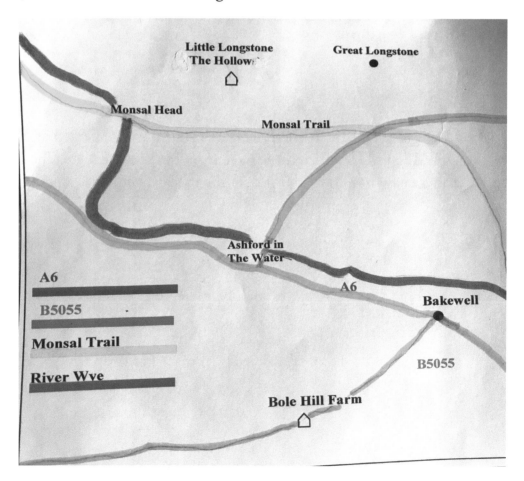

Sheepwash Bridge in Ashford:

Here is the famous **"Sheepwash Bridge;"** over the River Wye; a packhorse bridge where livestock crossed. On the picture to the right, there is a section at the end of the bridge where the lambs are herded and kept, so that the ewes would swim over to them getting washed in the process.

A pleasant stop in Ashford: We decided to stop for lunch at this delightful Riverside Hotel and café. Trevor is sitting there, waiting to give our order. It is always a pleasure to have afternoon tea or morning coffee while hiking or even lunch if the time is right. It is one of one of the pleasures of hiking in an area that has villages and a population.

Hiking all day in wilderness with no pit stops may be fine for some, but I prefer to get my fun, fitness and discovery without pain, privation and discomfort. Each to his own, I guess. For those that prefer a more outward bound experience, there is plenty of moorland hiking north of Castleton where the population is sparse and you can hike all day seeing no one.

BAKEWELL:

Bakewell is the de facto capital of the Peak District. The first recorded fair was held here in 1254. Its history however, goes further back to Bakewell's first known resident who was called "Badeca". Records show that in 924AD the local springs were named after him "Badeca's Well, hence "Bakewell". The 1000-year-old Market is still held every Monday. There are also two ancient bridges to ponder and explore. There is a lot of history here which makes it an interesting place to visit or to stay.

Many have heard of Bakewell but it is especially famous for its **"Bakewell Tart"** As a visitor, there are many shops and places to eat here and of course, it is the starting point for the **Monsal Trail** which officially begins at Bakewell station found on a minor road above Bakewell.

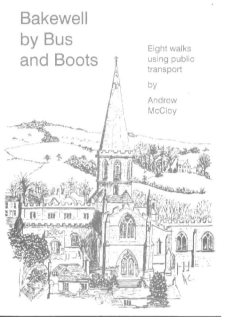

Bakewell by Bus and Boots

Eight walks using public transport

by Andrew McCloy

Since Bakewell is a hub, it is possible to walk from here and take the bus back rather than try for a circular walk. The booklet pictured outlines 8 walks from Bakewell which use public transportation to return to base. This is very useful to hikers. We have used public transportation on countless occasions and always feel fortunate when an area we have chosen to walk has available bus service. Do check on the current times since they change according to season. Taking a bus schedule with you is another useful tool to help you with your hiking. The relevant one is **"Peak District: Bus and Train Times"**. The bus station is located at Rutland Square in Bakewell in front of the Rutland Hotel.

HADDON HALL:

While we often choose to visit properties owned by the National Trust and English Heritage, we make exceptions when the appeal of the property exceeds our need to watch our pennies.

Haddon Hall is one of those must see properties. As I have mentioned previously, our desire to see places often rests with our experiences with the books we have read, the movies we have seen or the T.V. shows we have followed. Haddon Hall has doubled as **Thornfield Hall in two different adaptations of Jane Eyre** and has also appeared in several other films including, **"The Princess Bride" (1987) "Elizabeth" (1998), Pride and Prejudice (2005)** and **"The Other Boleyn Girl"(2008)** Since we were in an historical society for the Tudor time period for twenty years, seeing these film locations was definitely something on our list of places to see.

Haddon Hall has the most wonderful gardens. We have been there at least twice and the gardens are what I remember the most. They are spectacular and were in full bloom when we visited. My album is full of pictures of the flowers.

The hall itself is owned by the 11th Duke of Rutland, Lord Edward Manners. It lay unoccupied from the 18th Century until the early 20th century when the present Earl's grandfather returned to Haddon and set about restoring it to its current beauty. The gardens were created by his grandmother, the 9th Duchess of Rutland and they are indeed beautiful.

Haddon Hall is an example of a fortified manor house and presents a fine example of medieval and Tudor architecture.

As you wander through the rooms absorbing the details of the tapestries, the parlour, the Great Chamber, the Long Gallery, the kitchens, the chapel and all the other rooms that make up the lifestyle of the inhabitants of the manor house, it gives you a glimpse of history and how it has unfolded.

The gardens are the finishing touch to your visit to Haddon Hall. Such beautiful delphiniums!

We are very lucky to be able to witness history through the preservation of the homes from another age. People have taken the time to restore using their own resources to fund the project. This shows a respect for and appreciation of history as they gift their properties to the nation in the case of National Trust Properties, or the descendants make their inherited homes available to the public and continue to maintain these properties at a high level for our enjoyment.

DISCOVERING OTHER GEMS IN THE BAKEWELL AREA:

In planning a hiking holiday, you will obviously choose areas where the paths are plentiful. That is the first consideration along with some research on the appeal of the area. Part of the appeal is not only the hiking but whether there are other attractions available to visit. There are days when you don't hike, when you choose to visit attractions and walk on their properties instead of on trails. The ease of access to Bakewell brought us into the area where we discovered the wonderful hiking paths. What we also discovered was that it is an area of historical significance as well. We searched out Haddon Hall but we discovered many other places to visit which deserve a mention and a picture. I especially like places that teach us a little history, introduce us to historical heroes or widen our knowledge of the people and the land that we are exploring. The Peak District has many places worthy of mention.

1. Chatsworth House:

Chatsworth House is the stately home of the present Duke of Devonshire. The estate is extensive and the home magnificent. It too is associated with T.V. and film productions such as **"Pride and Prejudice"** in 2005 where Chatsworth represented Pemberley. **"The Duchess"** 2008 was also filmed here as was the BBC Production of the P.D. James book, **"Death Comes to Pemberly"** in 2013. It is considered one of Britain's finest stately homes. It is also set in "Chatsworth Park" which is one of the highlights of the Peak District. Here you will find 1000 acres of parkland and gardens, fallow deer and woodland trails. The house is visitor friendly with much to see for all age groups. It is privately owned so there is an admission charge.

Bakewell to Chatsworth is 4.5 miles - or a 10 minute drive.

Chatsworth House:

The 2005 version of Pride and Prejudice starred Keira Knightly, Mathew Macfadyen, Donald Sutherland and Dame Judi Dench. Pemberly (Chatsworth) is pictured above. A display on the film is found in Chatsworth and is pictured on the right.

2. Eyam, The Plague Village:

We found this village quite by accident as we were exploring around while in the Bakewell area. Due to our current situation with the Convid 19 pandemic where we are quarantined against the spread of the virus, the plight of this village is particularly relevant and worth writing about.

Bakewell to Eyam Village is 6.7 miles or a 13-minute drive

Eyam was a village that quarantined itself after an outbreak of Bubonic plague in 1665. The plague arrived in the village in a bale of cloth sent from London which was experiencing a severe outbreak of the disease. In the bale of damp cloth were fleas carrying the pestilence. As the bale was unpacked and hung to dry, the insects emerged and there it began. The tailor's assistant, George Viccars who had opened the bale, was the first to die. He was visiting Eyam to help make clothes for a religious festival and never left.

Between September and December 1665, 42 villagers died of the disease and by the spring of 1666, they were on the verge of fleeing their village to escape death.

However, their newly appointed vicar, William Mompesson, persuaded them to quarantine the village to avoid spreading the pestilence to the nearby towns of Bakewell and Sheffield. On June 24, 1666, Mompesson told his parishioners that the village must be enclosed with no one coming in or going out. The Earl of Devonshire, who lived nearby at Chatsworth had offered to send food and supplies if the villagers agreed to be quarantined.

Food and medicine were brought to this well and coins were left in the well in payment. Vinegar was added to disinfect the coins. (A bit like our no cash situation today in the shops that are open.)

The villagers reluctantly agreed to the quarantine. The decision to quarantine the village meant that human-to-human contact with those outside the village was eliminated which also prevented the spread of the disease to towns and villages nearby.

In the summer, which was very hot that year, the fleas were more active, and the number of victims increased. In August, one villager, Elizabeth Hancock, buried 6 of her children and her husband in the space of 8 days. Entire families were wiped out. The number of cases fell in September and October and by November 1, the disease had gone. Eyam's mortality rate exceeded that suffered by citizens of London. In just over a year, 260 villagers from 76 different families had died. Historians placed the total population of Eyam at between 350 and 800 before the plague struck.

This story is well known by the people of Eyam today with appreciation for what their ancestors did to prevent the spread of the disease while a third of them lost their lives by their sacrifice.

3. Nine Ladies Stone Circle:

Bakewell to Nine Ladies Stone Circle - 4.3 miles or a 11 minute drive.

This interesting historical site was an accidental find after we had eaten dinner in a local pub. It is located on Stanton Moor just south of Bakewell and is an English Heritage property. The stones date from the Bronze Age of 3000 - 4000 years ago.

As to the meaning of the circle, historians point to possibilities such as a meeting place, landmark, place of ceremony or burial but as none can be proved, it remains an historical mystery but also an interesting visit.

Here are two photos from the album of this historical site.

Bronze Age in the Peak District:

This area was well populated and farmed in the Bronze Age. Evidence of their habitation survives in henges such as Arbor Low near Youlgreave and Nine Ladies Stone Circle at Stanton Moor. In this period and into the Iron Age, Hill Forts such as the one at Mam Tor were created. Even earlier finds such as flint artifacts and evidence collected from caves has been discovered in the Dovedale region. The Romans inhabited Buxton which was known as "Aquae Arnemetiae," while they exploited the rich veins of lead in the area.

---

4. Lyme Park:

Bakewell to Lyme Park - 23.8 miles or a 44 minute drive

For Lyme Park we are going a little further afield but the trip is still under an hour. I am including this location as part of the "Pride and Prejudice" search for locations from their film productions.

This is a National Trust property so members will have free admission and parking.

For all those that remember Colin Firth's portrayal of Mr. Darcy and his impromptu swim in the lake, this is the location. While Elizabeth was touring his house, he returned early to his property and took his famous dip. This rather marked a turning point in their relationship when he encountered her as she emerged from the house.

For Jane Austin fans, this is a must-see location.

5. Hardwick Hall and Hardwick Old Hall:

Bakewell to Hardwick Hall - 21.3 miles or 37 minutes by car

As you can see from the map, this property is located just off the M1. This would be an excellent "en route" property to visit as you continue south from the Peak District. It is always pleasant to make worthwhile stops while on your way to your next accommodation or area of exploration.

Hardwick Hall is memorable for its appearance and its inhabitants. It has often been said that it is "more glass than wall" and when you look at it you can see why. The windows are its most notable feature. Also the huge initials ES crowning the roof line, proclaim this home to be the property of a formidable renaissance woman, **Bess of Hardwick** mentioned previously in the section on Buxton. Bess was born in 1527, the daughter of a Derbyshire Squire who had a small manor house at Hardwick. She was first married at 14, and was widowed four times. Each marriage advanced her social position and brought her wealth. Her last husband, the 6th Earl of Shrewbury, was head of one of the oldest, grandest and richest families in England. When Bess was 62, her fourth husband died which gave her access to his immense wealth. A month later she laid the foundations for **Hardwick Hall** a short distance from the still uncompleted Old Hall. She moved into her new home 7 years later and died there in 1608 at the age of 80.

Her "rags to riches" story which led her from modest beginnings to being the richest woman in England and the fact that she lived until 80, in an age when most women didn't make it past 40 is indeed remarkable. Hardwick Hall today survives with many of its original contents still in place as per the inventory taken in 1601.

Mary, Queen of Scots was imprisoned here which was a big factor in saving the home from neglect and decay in the subsequent years after Bess' death. One of Mary's hobbies during her incarceration was embroidery and I remember a room devoted to samples of her work. There is also an element of intrigue in the story of "Arabella Stuart", her granddaughter. Arabella, was a possible heir to Elizabeth's throne because her father was the Queen's cousin and brother-in-law of Mary Queen of Scots. She lived under her grandmother's tight rein until her late twenties but subsequently died in the tower after marrying a rival claimant to James' 1 throne.

Our daughter Angie is seen viewing the ruins of **Hardwick Old Hall** nearby.

6. Wingfield Manor:

Bakewell to Wingfield Manor - 15.7 miles or a 31-minute drive

Wingfield Manor is an English Heritage property which also continues with the Mary Queen of Scots theme. It is famous as the prison from which Anthony Babington plotted to rescue the imprisoned Queen. A book, *"A Traveller in Time"* by Alison Uttley, tells the story of the *Babington Plot* and makes an interesting read.

Anthony Babington was acquainted with Mary through his position as page in the Earl of Shrewsbury's household. He was young, catholic and was determined to rescue the Scottish Queen and replace Queen Elizabeth on the throne of England. By 1586, the plot was afoot. Walsingham, in the employment of Queen Elizabeth was aware of the plot, and had the correspondence between Mary and Babington monitored. Their letters contained incriminating evidence of treason which led to Mary's execution at Fotheringhay Castle and Babington's demise in the Tower of London.

The ruins have enough details to get a look at what the home would have been like when Mary was a prisoner there. A tour takes you through the various rooms and describes the history of this important location in the story of Mary, Queen of Scots.

7. Cromford Mills - The Arkwright Connection:
Bakewell to Cromford Mills - 10.8 miles or a 21-minute drive by car.

Cromford Mills is an important industrial heritage location. It is the site of the first water-powered cotton spinning mill, which was developed by Richard Arkwright in 1771. He built a 5 story mill with the help of two financial supporters and starting in 1772, he ran the mills day and night in two twelve hour shifts.

The first workers numbered 200 which exceeded the number that the locale could supply, so he brought in workers and housed them in nearby buildings. Most of the employees were women and children, some as young as 7 years old. The minimum age was later raised to 10 and the children were given six hours of education per week so that they could do the record keeping that their parents were unable to do.

The importance of this mill is part of the story of industrialization - this time in the cotton industry. Prior to this, the cottage industry reigned, with villagers weaving the cotton. This was the first time that the workplace was no longer in the home and women and children were employed outside of their residence. This was a major shift in society from home-based crafts to an outside, industrialized workplace.

The mill was located at **Cromford** because of the available water supply which was needed to run the water-powered cotton spinning mill. The mill finally ceased operation in the 19th century and the buildings were re-purposed. In 1979, the site was purchased by the Arkwright Society who set about the task of restoring it to its original state. Its importance is that it was the first successful cotton spinning factory which led to it being widely copied in other areas of the country.

Today the site has been declared a **UNESCO World Heritage Site** and has an extensive visitor centre which includes shops, galleries, restaurants and cafes.

Nearby is the Cromford Canal and Cromford Wharf which together linked Arkwright's Mill to other Midland and Northern cities. However, its use declined with the advancement of the railways.

Cromford Mills World Heritage Site. An interesting day trip if you are in the area.

Nearby, you will find the **High Peak Trail** if you want to hike after your exploration of the Cromford Mill area. This is a scene from the trail.

HIKING IN THE NORTH OF ENGLAND

Conclusion:

This ends our discovery of The Peak District. There is much more to see but this is merely a taste of the delights you will find both in "Hiking and in Discovering" in this area of England. The Peak District could be an *en route* to the north destination or a destination in itself. It all depends on your inclination and your holiday time. In our travels we used the Peak District to shorten the drive to the north and stayed in our three locations on route to and from the north. In 2006 we spent a full two weeks there and covered two of the three areas. We have visited many times and always find great places to hike and more things to see.

Why the North?

The North of England is often an area missed by organized tours. It remains undiscovered, pastoral and full of history. The hiking is well documented and has many circular walks described in detail in the Pathfinder Series. There are also the linear trails such as **The Dales Way, The Cleveland Way, A Coast to Coast Walk, The Hadrian's Wall Path and The Monsal Way** to name a few.

We enjoyed the North while our holiday time was in the summer because I was still teaching. **The accommodation is more reasonable in High Season** in the North, especially for cottage rentals. B&B's remain similar in price, but we were gradually moving towards cottage rental so that was a consideration.

The North in the summer is also less crowded and is cooler in July and August than in the South. The weather in most of our holidays was delightful, the roads quiet, and the hiking superb.

The North was also where we learned to hike, bought our gear and became comfortable with following guides and learning to read the Ordinance Survey Maps.

It made an excellent training ground for hiking. There are varied landscapes, from Moorland to the Dales to the Lakes and to a variety of all three in the Peak District.

If you want crowds, excitement and an urban experience, there is York and also the Potteries in the Peak. There are also the smaller towns in the Lakes and the Moors which are equally interesting.

Entertainment and the North:

T.V. Shows: The Yorkshire Dales is the setting for the T.V Series **"All Creatures Great and Small"** mentioned in the book. There is a new series on PBS with new characters but the same theme and based on the previous series.

The movie . "**Miss Potter**" is the story of Beatrice Potter who is the hero of the Lake District. It stars Rene Zellwigger as Beatrice Potter. "**North and South**" is a story of the Cotton Industry and Richard Arkwright.

And so, we leave the North to discover other areas of Britain. In the time spent in **The Lake District, The Yorkshire Dales, the Yorkshire Moors, and the Peak District,** we have learned much. The journey for us took about 5 years and since we are visitors from Canada, this amounted to 5 months of hiking since each holiday was for a month.

We started exploring the North as novices and newcomers. We had done little hiking, relied heavily on the car and were choosing traditional forms of accommodation such as B&B's when we started our journey. At the end of this time period, we were hikers with all the gear. We were able to hike long distances using maps and guides and not get lost. We were using the car less and less and choosing to stay in cottages and self-cater which meant we were shopping for food and preparing our own. We were booking our accommodation prior to our arrival and sightseeing en route usually between our accommodations. Our focus was entirely on discovering and hiking. We had no fixed agenda, no list of tourist sites to see and were looking out and exploring places as we discovered them.

This new perspective was exciting. We felt part of the landscape during our visits and the thrill of discovering new places never ceased to please us. Our hikes were primarily circular ones which is why "**The Dales Way**" remains uncompleted as we have yet to figure out how to do a long stretch in the middle through moorland without doing an overnight on route. Considering that we are seniors, it seems unlikely that The Dales Way will be finished but that's OK. Our memories are all good.

Our journey in the North, also set us up for our future hiking challenges which we now felt were possible. The year 2000 ushered in new perspectives as we tentatively tackled the South West Coastal Path which was to become our next big challenge but not yet. We still had a way to go, mentally as much as physically.

"If you think you can do it, you probably can."

That was the perspective that was our next goal. Until then, hiking for fun, fresh air, enjoyment and good health was our commitment.

HAPPY HIKING

76

THE JOYS OF HIKING:

As an appendix to this book, let's define what we mean by hiking or define people's cultural perceptions of it. I personally had no definition of it in the early years since I had never done it. The 70's ushered in a time when I began taking my Grade 5-6 class into the Gatineau Hills in the fall for a walk around Pink's Lake. This constituted my early version of hiking. *It was walking outdoors, in nature and on trails as opposed to walking on sidewalks in urban areas.*

This definition has primarily remained even though our experiences have added other elements to it. Hiking here in the Ottawa area is usually limited to one day events. In good weather you use the time to head out on the nature trails that are nearby. It is a "one of" experience, not integrated with other activities.

Our vision has expanded through our experiences in England and this is mainly because the infrastructure in England supports an expanded version of hiking. We now realize that hiking can be a means of transportation and a journey of discovery both of the landscape and of ourselves. It is not simply a "day out."

With many long-distance paths, linked bus routes, plus maps and guides available, it is possible to plan circular or linear routes which cover several miles over varied terrain while discovering hitherto unknown historical sites en route. It is not a predictable hike through the forest for a couple of hours and back again.

Another version of hiking, perhaps more familiar to North Americans is the extreme version of hiking long distances found in hiking the *Appalachian Trail (2,190 miles)* or the *West Coast Trail. (75 km)* These versions of hiking often require camping out, carrying large packs and navigating challenging terrain. They would indeed give you a sense of accomplishment but would require a higher level of fitness than the average day hiker. Closer to home we have *The Bruce Trail (900 km)* in Southern Ontario and the *Rideau Trail (387 km)* between Ottawa and Kingston. There are other trails, but Canada is a large country and the trails are often far away and hard to reach which, for us, is a deterrent to experiencing them.

They also don't provide us with the experiences that we have come to enjoy - the cultural experience which adds to the overall satisfaction of hiking that we have enjoyed. The discovery aspect relating to history is a very important part of our joy of hiking. Our distances, our weather, and our sparse population would give us an entirely different experience from the one we have come to relish and will continue to do as long as we are able.

The following pages represent the viewpoints on hiking kindly offered by friends and acquaintances from their own experiences. I have started the observations with a personal list of *"Why we love Hiking in England"*.

Why We love hiking in England.... *Linda L.*

We started hiking in middle age, so our perspectives include sleeping in a bed at night and hiking on friendly and doable paths in lovely countryside. We find unlimited opportunities to hike this way in England. Short distances, many friendly paths well documented with maps and written information and always a chance to stop for refreshments in little villages or pubs. We love the moderate weather, not too hot or too cold and we are not besieged by biting insects so common in our forest walks here. The wildlife is friendly as are the people we meet. But most of all, we can combine a love of nature, hiking and being outdoors, with discovering the history of the area. We can usually find historical sites and buildings that enrich our knowledge of the culture and the history of the area and all within walking distance. It is an introduction into Cultural Geography. We hike, we enjoy, we learn and it is delightful.

A Perspective on Hiking ..... *Carolyn Andrews, Ottawa*

There is so much to see and do as we travel through life. Getting outside to explore, to discover places unknown to me or to revisit the familiar has inspired me to hike, walk or run as a part of my every day.

Hiking is a "pragmatic" activity - the simplicity and ease of it while keeping my body and brain healthy, combined with its minimal cost, makes it so. Yet it brings so much pleasure, even joy to my life. I love to plan for where I'll walk the following day and then enjoy the outcome. When travelling, there is no better way to see a hillside, a wooded terrain, a beach wherever I may be, than to hike and explore on foot. In a city, I love to walk through the downtown, through neighbourhoods and parks so I can see the architecture, meet people and feel the culture and personality of that city.

Today, while staying in a cabin in rural Newfoundland, I am planning a mid-winter walk on a snowmobile trail in the woods. I will see the trees, the hills and the ocean. I might see wildlife and I expect to feel peaceful and happy. I love hiking as an essential part of my everyday life.

A Persective on Hiking - *Susan Miller, England.*

In 2006, Dennis (hubby) and I went to London for our 20th Anniversary. While strolling down Oxford St. we nipped into an outdoor shop to buy a rucksack to put our carrier bags in, thereby freeing up our hands.

About 30 minutes later Dennis said,

"Oh, I like this walking lark, maybe we should do it proper", to which

I replied, "What do you mean proper?"

Susan and Dennis

"Well, the kids are grown up (youngest was 16) and we should spend a bit of time together on my days off."

I said, "We could both do with losing a bit of weight so Yeah, why not?"

He then suggested a "Proper Walk" would be something like **Hadrian's Wall.** I had NO idea where or what it was, but agreed to do some research when we got back home to Wigan, N.W. England. That was in August 2006.

By January 2007 we had started going out for local walks every Monday and Tuesday. It got us both out of the house; it was great spending time together and we talked and talked. We started with one hour at a time and increased it weekly until we were having full days out, with picnic lunches. We had built up to 12-mile walks and were both loving it.

We knew from our research that we would need to walk at least 14/15 miles per day for a week to complete Hadrian's Wall so we started catching buses and trains and going for rougher terrain. Our Leeds and Liverpool canal walks were mostly flat. By August 2007 we were ready and set off on our first walking holiday adventure.

It was fabulous. It was hard in places but we totally enjoyed it. We had to carry a rucksack each with waterproofs, food, drink etc. but most of our luggage was taken by minibus to our next B&B. Each night was a new place, most served evening meals but one didn't. Instead, they drove us to the next village with a pub which served food.

We met loads of other walkers each day on a route that was easy to follow but like a roller coaster, up and down, at times. At the end of the week, we had walked 93 miles and were super happy and proud of ourselves.

We expanded our perspectives to the Lake District and have climbed 30 of Wainwright's suggested peaks. We have been to the Lakes every year since our first time. In 2015, I saw the 1000-mile challenge in the Country Walking magazine and the first year did manage to do 990 miles without any help. I was gutted not to have made it to 1000. In 2016, the Facebook group started and everyone was friendly and supportive and encouraging. New friends, new hiking goals and new adventures.

Hiking and Better Health: *Ginny Hall, Mahone Bay, Nova Scotia*

I was getting frustrated by my health issues and two hip replacements that were keeping me stuck in a rut of disability. I decided to change.

A possible trip to Newfoundland with my husband was the push I needed. I had read about a unique fiord and wished to see it. However, the only way to get to it involved a 3.5 km hike. I decided to try short walks with that goal in mind. At first it was slow and gradual. It took three months of daily walking before I could cover the distances and feel the positives. I could go further without too much blowback and I felt that progress was begin made. Once I had attained my goal, I just kept on walking because I, as well as others, recognize that both my physical and mental state have improved. Where before, I looked for ways to justify my not doing it, now I looked for ways of doing it - no excuses. I became positive instead of limiting. I have learned that walking was certainly a major contributor to my better health, both physical and mental and that is a big plus for me.

Walking in the Urban Setting: *Catherine Reynolds - Ottawa, Ontario*

I was born in France and spent my first 21 years walking everywhere; to the shops, visiting friends and on the beach.

Later when I moved to Montreal, I walked everywhere to become familiar with the city. I also enjoyed discovering a city by foot which allows me to stop and talk to people.

I moved to Ottawa and since I worked downtown, I would use every opportunity to walk - at lunch along the canal or on Parliament Hill and it became a way to stay healthy and to relieve stress.

During the pandemic, I have discovered the fields around our home. I take long walks there as a way to meditate, contemplate and centre my body, mind, heart and spirit.

I just love walking and as I am growing older, I am so much more aware of its health benefits and will continue to walk as long as I am able.

Why I Love Hiking - *Sally Tronina, Porthcawl, Wales*

Hiking is a huge part of my life and keeps me healthy; physically, mentally and emotionally. In addition to the health benefits, I have always had the need to discover new places and enjoy an adventure. Hiking allows that to happen.

I try to walk the Gower coastal path every year as it is a physical challenge which means I come away with such a feeling of gratitude and accomplishment. Its paths vary and can change depending on what a battering the landscape has taken over the year. The sea is blue and you can often find a seal basking or dolphins putting on a display. It is a peaceful hike and you may not see another person for hours which is what I enjoy the most.

I think a hike can mean many things. It can be a 2 mile walk in the sand to 15 miles on path or pavement but as long as it's your journey and you are enjoying it, that is what is ultimately important.

I will continue to hike until my legs say no because that's when I'm most alive.

My Love of Hiking Goes Way Back: *Trevor Whitwam - Ottawa, Ont.*

As a boy, I often went on rambles with my parents across the Yorkshire Moors. As a teenager, I continued walking with my friends across trackless moors with the way marked by cairns but I never knew the spectacular scenery and views of walking in the Yorkshire Dales.

This came later, much later. I emigrated to Canada, had a career and a family and finally started having annual vacations back to England with a new wife. Now that I had the time, the resources and the companion, I could plan excursions in and around the Dales, both Yorkshire and Derbyshire. I discovered the beauty of the Dales by walking the trails around Kettlewell and Grassington. I found the fresh air, the scenery and the exercise made my vacations memorable especially as I was accompanied by Linda, my partner who also enjoyed walking in the Dales. Together, we made memories over the years which we still cherish to this day. Hiking is fun but hiking with a companion makes it more so. You can share the experience, the stories and the photos years later and that makes it especially appealing for couples. It is something that they share and that makes it special.

AUTHORS NOTE:

Thank you for reading my book on the North of England. I hope you found it illuminating. The North is really the forgotten part of England. Apart from the Lake District and the City of York, the other areas are generally enjoyed by the locals rather than those from away.

Yorkshire, The Lakes and the Peak District are showcases for the northern National Parks which have preserved the landscape and the cultural tone of the area giving you a glimpse of life as it used to be. This is especially true if you hike. Driving by in a car you simply glimpse historical sites. Hiking to them gives you a deeper insight into the past and a greater satisfaction of discovery.

This is an ideal place to start to hike as we did. It helped develop our desire and ability to take to the trails and also gave us the confidence to do so. Without our experience in the North, I doubt that we would have attempted later challenges such as hiking the entire South West Coastal Path.

We have found that a hiking holiday is an ideal "couple holiday". Hiking with a young family would be difficult. We hiked with our adult daughters and enjoyed the experience, because their ability matched our own.

For older adults whose family has grown, it is ideal. Walking is considered one of the healthiest pursuits. It is physically and mentally rejuvenating and as a couple it gives you a shared interest to pursue which is often difficult to find once the family has grown up and gone their separate ways. We see many couples in England hiking and often stop to chat with them. This shared pursuit is important to them. A day hiking in nature followed by afternoon tea or a stop in a café is a rewarding way to spend time together.

In England, where the opportunities abound for hiking, one can ponder the possibilities of this type of holiday since the infrastructure supports it. We feel grateful to have discovered hiking and hope you will too.

Bibliography of Books on Hiking:

Title: Author

1. *A Walk in the Woods*   Bill Bryson

   A story of Bill Bryson's experiences when he walked on the Appalachian Trail.

2. *The Old Ways*   Robert MacFarlane

   A clever book about walking, set in landscapes in the British countryside.

3. *City of York,*   Linda Loder

   Guides to Exploring England Independently

4. *Notes from a Small Island*   Bill Bryson

   Walking Around Britain

5. *The Kingdom by the Sea*   Paul Theroux

   My first introduction to hiking in England.

6. *The Road to Little Dribbling*   Bill Bryson

   Another amusing account of Hiking and travelling in England

References Used in our Northern Hiking Adventures:

1. The Dales Way   Anthony Burton
2. The Walker's Guide to Wharfedale   A. David Leather
3. The Yorkshire Dales   Marie Hartley and Joan Ingilby
4. Discovering the Yorkshire Dales   John Ward
5. North York Moors Walks   Pathfinder Guide -
6. Cleveland Way   Ian Sampson
7. James Herriot's Yorkshire   Derry Brabbs
8. A.A. 100 Weekend Walks in Britain   Introduction - Paul Sterry
9. Towns and Villages of Yorkshire   Alan Bryant
10. The Peak District Walks   Pathfinder Guide
11. Bakewell by Bus and Boots   Andrew McCloy
12. 8 Walks Around the Monsal Trail   Jim Rubery
13. Derbyshire Ghosts and Legends   David Bell
14. Haddon Hall   Bryan Cleary
15. The Making of Pride and Prejudice   Sue Birtwistle & Susie Conklin
16. Lakeland Footsteps of William Wordsworth Lindsay Porter
17. Walker's Companion - Lake District   Colin Shelbouorn
18. Beatrix Potter   The Pitkin Guide

CPSIA information can be obtained
at www.ICGtesting.com
Printed in the USA
BVHW020952280621
610635BV00002B/6